# Pas                    es

Please return/renew this item by the last date shown.

To renew this item, call **0845 0020777** (automated) or visit **www.librarieswest.org.uk**

Borrower number and PIN required.

LibrariesWest

**Good Housekeeping**

# easy to make!
# Pasta & Noodles

COLLINS & BROWN

First published in Great Britian in 2012
by Collins & Brown
10 Southcombe Street
London W14 0RA

An imprint of Anova Books Company Ltd

The Good Housekeeping website is
www.goodhousekeeping.co.uk

10 9 8 7 6 5 4 3 2 1

ISBN 978-1-908449-10-8

A catalogue record for this book is available from the British
Library.

Reproduction by Dot Gradations Ltd
Printed and bound by Times Printing, Malaysia

This book can be ordered direct from the publisher at
www.anovabooks.com

## NOTES

- Both metric and imperial measures are given for the recipes. Follow either set of measures, not a mixture of both, as they are not interchangeable.
- All spoon measures are level.
  1 tsp = 5ml spoon; 1 tbsp = 15ml spoon.
- Ovens and grills must be preheated to the specified temperature.
- Use sea salt and freshly ground black pepper unless otherwise suggested.
- Fresh herbs should be used unless dried herbs are specified in a recipe.
- Medium eggs should be used except where otherwise specified. Free-range eggs are recommended.
- Note that certain recipes, including mayonnaise, lemon curd and some cold desserts, contain raw or lightly cooked eggs. The young, elderly, pregnant women and anyone with an immune-deficiency disease should avoid these, because of the slight risk of salmonella.
- Calorie, fat and carbohydrate counts per serving are provided for the recipes.

### Picture Credits
Photographers: Neil Barclay (pages 51, 67, 89, 93 and 94); Steve
Baxter (page 38); Martin Brigdale (pages 41, 42, 44, 45, 57, 60,
61, 62, 70, 71, 74, 88, 92, 98, 100, 101, 120, 122, 123 and 125);
Nicki Dowey (pages 32, 33, 35, 40 ,49, 52, 53, 55, 56, 58, 66, 73,
78, 79, 81, 82, 84, 87, 95, 97, 102, 103, 106, 107, 110, 111, 112,
113, 114, 118, 119 and 126); Craig Robertson (all Basics
photography and pages 59, 72 and 83); Lucinda Symons (pages
34, 37, 39, 48, 50, 69, 86, 109 and 117)
Stylists: Wei Tang, Helen Trent and Fanny Ward
Home Economists: Joanna Farrow, Emma Jane Frost, Teresa
Goldfinch, Alice Hart, Lucy McKelvie, Kim Morphew and Mari
Mererid Williams

# Contents

# Foreword

Cooking, for me, is one of life's great pleasures. Not only is it necessary to fuel your body, but it exercises creativity, skill, social bonding and patience. The science behind the cooking also fascinates me, learning to understand how yeast works, or to grasp why certain flavours marry quite so well (in my mind) is to become a good cook.

I've often encountered people who claim not to be able to cook – they're just not interested or say they simply don't have time. My sister won't mind me saying that she was one of those who sat firmly in the camp of disinterested domestic goddess. But things change, she realised that my mother (an excellent cook) can't always be on hand to prepare steaming home-cooked meals and that she actually wanted to become a mother one day who was able to whip up good food for her own family. All it took was some good cook books (naturally, Good Housekeeping was present and accounted for) and some enthusiasm and sure enough she is now a kitchen wizard, creating such confections that even baffle me.

I've been lucky enough to have had a love for all things culinary since as long as I can remember. Baking rock-like chocolate cakes and misshapen biscuits was a right of passage that I protectively guard. I made my mistakes young, so have lost the fear of cookery mishaps. I think it's these mishaps that scare people, but when you realise that a mistake made once will seldom be repeated, then kitchen domination can start.

This Good Housekeeping Easy to Make! collection is filled with hundreds of tantalising recipes that have been triple tested (at least!) in our dedicated test kitchens. They have been developed to be easily achievable, delicious and guaranteed to work – taking the chance out of cooking.

I hope you enjoy this collection and that it inspires you to get cooking.

*Meike.*

Meike Beck
Cookery Editor
Good Housekeeping

# O

# The Basics

# Making fresh pasta

Although you can buy good-quality fresh pasta, it's easy and fun to make it at home. And while a pasta machine will make quick work of rolling and cutting, you can do it all by hand.

## Fresh pasta

To make pasta to serve three to four people, you will need: 300–400g (11–14oz) flour (see Cook's Tips), 4 medium eggs, beaten, 1 tbsp extra virgin olive oil.

**1** Sift 300g (11oz) flour on to a clean worksurface. Make a well in the centre, then add the eggs and oil. Draw in the flour until the mixture resembles breadcrumbs.

**2** When the flour and eggs are combined, knead the dough for 5–10 minutes until smooth and elastic. Wrap in clingfilm and leave to rest for 1 hour.

**3** Dust the dough and worksurface with flour and roll out the dough until you can see the worksurface through it.

**4** Hang the pasta over a rolling pin and leave it to dry on the board until it no longer feels damp, then cut it (see opposite).

## Herb pasta

Sift the flour and salt into the bowl and stir in 3 tbsp freshly chopped mixed herbs, such as basil, marjoram and parsley. Continue as for the basic pasta dough.

## Cook's Tips

**For the best results,** use Italian '00' strong flour.
**When you're rolling out** the pasta, have something ready to hang it on while it dries – a clothes airer or a rolling pin is perfect for this.

## Cutting pasta with a knife

**1** Lay the sheet of dough on a floured worksurface and dust lightly with flour. Lift one edge and fold it over, then keep folding to make a long, flat cigar-shape.

**2** Cut the dough into strips of the required width. Unfold and leave them to dry on a clean teatowel for a few minutes before cooking.

## Using a pasta machine

**1** Make the pasta dough (see left) to the end of step 2. Cut the dough into small pieces that will fit through the machine's rollers. Dust the pasta with flour. Set the rollers as wide apart as they will go, then feed the dough through. Repeat two or three times, folding the dough into three after each roll.

**2** Narrow the rollers and repeat. Continue until the pasta is of the right thickness, then cut as required.

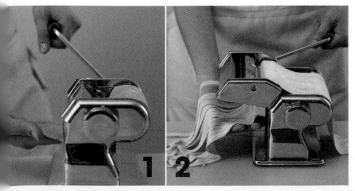

## Filling ravioli

**1** Lay a sheet of dough over a ravioli tray and gently press it into the indentations. Place teaspoonfuls of filling into the hollows. Be particularly careful not to overfill the ravioli, as the filling may leak out during cooking. Lay a second sheet of pasta on top of the first.

**2** Using a wheel cutter, cut the rows vertically between the lumps of filling in one direction, then cut horizontally in the other direction to make squares. Press the edges to seal the dough.

**3** Separate the ravioli, dust very lightly with flour and cover with a clean teatowel until needed. This will help prevent the ravioli from drying out while you are making more of them.

## Making filled pasta shapes

**1** Make the pasta dough (see left) to the end of step 2. Cut the dough into small pieces and roll out just one piece at a time. Keep the rest covered in clingfilm to prevent it from drying out.

**2** Trim one edge to make a straight line, then cut a strip about 5cm (2in) from the straight edge. Cut into pieces about 5cm (2in) square.

**3** Place a teaspoonful of filling at the centre of one square, then fold over to make a triangle. Do not overfill. Press the edges to seal.

**4** Fold the topmost corner of the triangle down, then fold the other two edges over to leave a hollow space in the middle of the pasta. Press the two folded corners together firmly. Repeat with the remaining pasta and filling.

# Cooking pasta

The popular staples of pasta and noodles can transform meat, poultry, fish and vegetable dishes into substantial meals. Perfectly cooked pasta and noodles make super-quick accompaniments; noodles can also be added to stir-fried dishes as one of the ingredients.

## Cooking pasta

There are a number of mistaken ideas about cooking pasta, such as adding oil to the water, rinsing the pasta after cooking and adding salt only at a certain point. The basics couldn't be simpler. Add salt to the water before adding the pasta. Filled pasta is the only type of pasta that needs oil in the cooking water – the oil reduces friction, which could tear the wrappers and allow the filling to come out. Use 1 tbsp for a large pan of water. Rinse the pasta after cooking only if you are going to cool it for serving as salad, then drain well and toss with oil.

### Dried pasta

**1** Heat the water with about 1 tsp salt per 100g (3½oz) of pasta. Bring to a rolling boil, then put in all the pasta and stir well for 30 seconds, to keep the pasta from sticking.

**2** Once the water is boiling again, set the timer for 2 minutes less than the cooking time on the pack and cook uncovered. Check the pasta when the timer goes off, then every 60 seconds until it is cooked al dente: tender, but with a little bite at the centre.

**3** Drain the pasta in a colander. Toss with your chosen sauce.

### Fresh pasta

Fresh pasta is cooked in the same way as dried, but for a shorter time.

**1** Bring the water to the boil. Add the pasta to the boiling water all at once and stir well. Set the timer for 2 minutes and keep testing every 30 seconds until the pasta is cooked al dente: tender, but with a little bite at the centre.

# Basic sauces

## Bolognese Sauce

**To serve six, you will need:**
2 tbsp olive oil, 1 onion, finely chopped, 2 garlic cloves, crushed, 450g (1lb) extra-lean minced beef, 2 tbsp sun-dried tomato paste, 300ml (½ pint) red wine, 400g can chopped tomatoes, 125g (4oz) chestnut mushrooms, sliced, 2 tbsp Worcestershire sauce, salt and ground black pepper.

**1** Heat the oil in a large pan, add the onion and fry over a medium heat for 10 minutes until softened and golden. Add the garlic and cook for 1 minute.

**2** Add the beef and brown evenly, using a wooden spoon to break up the pieces. Stir in the tomato paste and wine, cover and bring to the boil. Add the tomatoes, mushrooms and Worcestershire sauce and season well with salt and pepper. Bring back to the boil, lower the heat and simmer for 20 minutes.

## Classic Tomato Sauce

**To serve four, you will need:**
1 tbsp olive oil, 1 small onion, chopped, 1 carrot, grated, 1 celery stick, chopped, 1 garlic clove, crushed, ½ tbsp tomato purée, 2 x 400g cans plum tomatoes, 1 bay leaf, ½ tsp oregano, 2 tsp caster sugar, 3 tbsp freshly chopped basil, salt and ground black pepper.

**1** Heat the oil in a large pan. Add the onion, carrot and celery and fry gently for 20 minutes until softened.

**2** Add the garlic and tomato purée to the pan and fry for 1 minute. Stir in the tomatoes and add the bay leaf, oregano and sugar. Simmer for 30 minutes until thickened.

**3** Stir the basil into the sauce and check the seasoning.

## Pesto

**To serve four, you will need:**
50g (2oz) fresh basil leaves, roughly torn, 1–2 garlic cloves, 25g (1oz) pinenuts, 6 tbsp extra virgin olive oil, 2 tbsp freshly grated Parmesan, lemon juice (optional), salt and ground black pepper.

**1** Put the basil in a food processor with the garlic, pinenuts and 2 tbsp olive oil. Blend to a fairly smooth paste. Gradually add the remaining oil and season.

**2** Transfer to a bowl and stir in the Parmesan. Add a squeeze of lemon juice if you like. Store in the refrigerator: cover with a thin layer of olive oil and seal tightly. It will keep for up to three days.

### Variations

**Coriander Pesto** Use fresh coriander instead of basil; add 1 seeded, finely chopped chilli in step 1. Omit the cheese.
**Rocket Pesto** Replace the basil with rocket leaves and add 1 tbsp freshly chopped parsley.
**Sun-dried Tomato Pesto** Replace half the basil with 50g (2oz) sun-dried tomatoes, drained of oil and chopped.

## Béchamel Sauce

**To make 300ml (½ pint), you will need:**
1 onion slice, 6 peppercorns, 1 mace blade, 1 bay leaf, 15g (½ oz) butter, 15g (½ oz) plain flour, salt and ground black pepper, freshly grated nutmeg

**1** Pour the milk into a pan. Add the onion slice, peppercorns, mace and bay leaf. Bring almost to the boil, remove from the heat, and cover and leave to infuse for about 20 minutes, then strain.

**2** To make the roux, melt the butter in a pan, stir in the flour and cook, stirring, for 1 minute until cooked but not coloured.

**3** Remove from the heat and gradually pour on the infused milk, whisking constantly. Season lightly with salt, pepper and grated nutmeg.

**4** Return to the heat and cook, stirring constantly, until the sauce is thickened and smooth. Simmer gently for 2 minutes.

# Cooking noodles

## Egg (wheat) noodles

These are the most versatile of Asian noodles. Like Italian pasta, they are made from wheat flour, egg and water, and are available fresh or dried in various thicknesses.

**1** Bring a pan of water to the boil and put the noodles in.

**2** Agitate the noodles using chopsticks or a fork to separate them. This can take a minute or even more.

**3** Continue boiling for 4–5 minutes until the noodles are cooked al dente: tender but with a little bite at the centre.

**4** Drain well and then rinse in cold water and toss with a little oil if you are not using them immediately.

## Glass, cellophane or bean thread noodles

These very thin noodles are made from mung beans; they need only 1 minute in boiling water.

## Rice noodles

These may be very fine (rice vermicelli) or thick and flat. Most need no cooking, only soaking in warm or hot water; check the packet instructions, or cover the noodles with freshly boiled water and soak until they are al dente: tender but with a little bite at the centre. Drain well and toss with a little oil if you are not using them immediately.

## Perfect noodles

Use 50–75g (2–3oz) uncooked noodles per person.
**Dried egg noodles** are often packed in layers. As a general rule, allow one layer per person for a main dish.
**If you plan to re-cook the noodles** after the initial boiling or soaking – for example, in a stir-fry – it's best to undercook them slightly.
**When cooking a layer,** block or nest of noodles, use a pair of forks or chopsticks to untangle the strands from the moment they go into the water.

  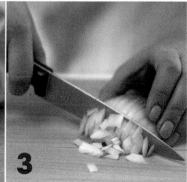

# Preparing vegetables

Just a few basic techniques will help you to prepare all these frequently used vegetables ready for quick cooking in your pasta, noodle and rice dishes.

## Onions

**1** Cut off the tip and base of the onion. Peel away all the layers of papery skin and any discoloured layers underneath.

**2** Put the onion, root-end down, on the chopping board, then, using a sharp knife, cut the onion in half from tip to base.

**3** **Slicing** Put one half on the board, with the cut surface facing down, and slice across the onion.

**4** **Chopping** Slice the halved onions, from the root end to the top, at regular intervals. Next, make 2–3 horizontal slices through the onion, then slice vertically across the width.

## Shallots

**1** Cut off the tip and trim off the ends of the root. Peel off the skin and any discoloured layers underneath.

**2** Holding the shallot root-end down, use a sharp knife to make deep parallel slices almost down to the base, while keeping the slices attached to it.

**3** **Slicing** Turn the shallot on its side and cut off slices from the base.

**4** **Dicing** Make deep parallel slices at right angles to the first slices. Turn the shallot on its side and cut off the slices from the base. You should now have fine dice, but chop any larger pieces individually.

## Leeks

As some leeks harbour a lot of grit and earth between their leaves, they need careful cleaning.

**1** Cut off the root and any tough parts. Make a cut into the leaf end of the leek, about 7.5cm (3in) deep.

**2** Hold under the cold tap while separating the cut halves to expose any grit. Wash well, then shake dry. Slice or cut into matchsticks.

## Pak choi

Also known as bok choy, pak choi is a type of cabbage that does not form a heart. It has dark green leaves and thick, fleshy white stalks, which are sometimes cooked separately.

## Mushrooms

Button, white, chestnut and flat mushrooms are all prepared in a similar way.

**1** Wipe with a damp cloth or pastry brush to remove any dirt.

**2** Button mushrooms: cut off the stalk flush with the base of the cap. Other mushrooms: cut a thin disc off the end of the stalk and discard. Chop or slice the mushrooms.

## Cabbage

The crinkly-leaved Savoy cabbage may need more washing than other varieties, because its open leaves catch dirt more easily than the tightly packed white or red cabbage. The following method is suitable for all cabbages, including mild-flavoured Chinese leaves or Chinese cabbage.

**1** Pick off dry, discoloured or tough leaves. Cut off the base. Using a sharp knife, cut out as much as possible of the inner core in a single cone-shaped piece.

**2** If you need whole cabbage leaves, peel them off one by one. As you work your way down, you will need to cut out more of the core.

**3** If you are cooking the cabbage in wedges, cut it in half lengthways, then cut the pieces into wedges of the required size.

## Shredding cabbage

Cut the cabbage into quarters, then slice with a large cook's knife.

## Broccoli

**1** Slice off the end of the stalk and cut 1cm (½in) below the florets. Cut the broccoli head in half.

**2** Peel the thick, woody skin from the stalks and slice the stalks in half or quarters lengthways. Cut off equal-sized florets with a small knife. If the florets are very large, or if you want them for a stir-fry, you can halve them by cutting lengthways through the stalk and pulling the two halves apart.

## Carrots

**1** **Paring ribbons** Cut off the ends, then, using a vegetable peeler, peel off the skin and discard. Continue peeling the carrot into ribbon strips.

**2** **Slicing** Cut slices off each of the rounded sides to make four flat surfaces that are stable on the chopping board. Hold steady with one hand, and cut lengthways into even slices so they are lying in a flat stack. The stack can then be cut into batons or matchsticks.

## Asparagus

**1** Cut or snap off the woody stem of each asparagus spear about 5cm (2in) from the stalk's end, or where the white and green sections meet. Or cut off the stalk's end and peel with a vegetable peeler or small, sharp knife.

### Perfect vegetables
- - - - - - - - - - - - - - - - - - - - - - - - - - - - - - - - - - - - - -
**Wash vegetables** before you cut them up, to retain as many nutrients as possible.
**Cook as soon as possible** after you have cut them.
**Do not overcook** vegetables or they will lose their bright colour, crisp texture and some of their nutrients.

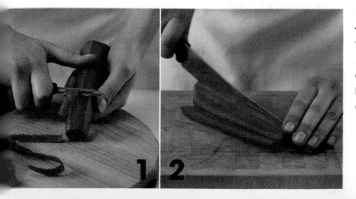

## Cutting tomatoes

**1** Use a small, sharp knife to cut out the core in a single cone-shaped piece. Discard the core.

**2** **Wedges** Halve the tomato and then cut into quarters or into three.

**3** **Slices** Hold the tomato with the cored side on the chopping board for greater stability and use a serrated knife to cut into slices.

## Seeding tomatoes

**1** Halve the tomato through the core. Use a spoon or a small, sharp knife to remove the seeds and juice. Shake off the excess liquid.

**2** Chop the tomato as required for your recipe and place in a colander for a minute or two, to drain off any excess liquid.

## Peeling tomatoes

**1** Fill a bowl or pan with boiling water. Using a slotted spoon, carefully add the tomato and leave for 15–30 seconds, then remove to a chopping board.

**2** Use a small, sharp knife to cut out the core in a single cone-shaped piece. Discard the core.

**3** Peel off the skin; it should come away easily, depending on ripeness.

## Avocados

Prepare avocados just before serving, because their flesh discolours quickly once exposed to air.

**1** Halve the avocado lengthways and twist the two halves apart. Tap the stone with a sharp knife, then twist to remove the stone.

**2** Run a knife between the flesh and skin and pull the skin away. Slice the flesh.

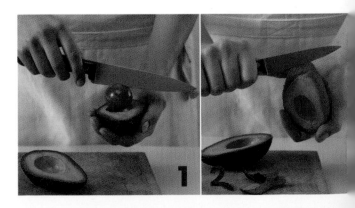

# Seeding peppers

The seeds and white pith of peppers taste bitter, so should be removed.

**1** Cut off the top of the pepper, then cut away and discard the seeds and white pith.

**2** Alternatively, cut the pepper in half vertically and snap out the white pithy core and seeds. Trim away the rest of the white membrane with a knife.

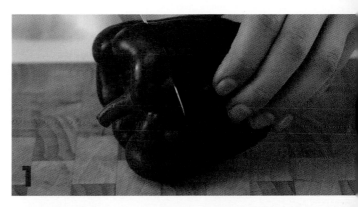

# Chargrilling peppers

Charring imparts a smoky flavour and makes peppers easier to peel.

**1** Hold the pepper, using tongs, over the gas flame on your hob (or put under a preheated grill) until the skin blackens, turning until black all over.

**2** Put in a bowl, cover and leave to cool (the steam will help to loosen the skin). Peel.

# Courgettes

Cutting on a diagonal is ideal for courgettes and other vegetables in a stir-fry.

**1** **2**

# Growing your own sprouted beans

Mung beans are the most commonly used sprouted beans for stir-fries, but chickpeas, green or Puy lentils and alfalfa are equally good and easy for home sprouting.

## Sprouting beans

You will only need about 3 tbsp beans to sprout at one time.

**1** Pick through the beans to remove any grit or stones, then soak in cold water for at least 8 hours. Drain and place in a clean (preferably sterilized) jar. Cover the top with a dampened piece of clean cloth, secure and leave in a warm, dark place.

**2** Rinse the sprouting beans twice a day. The sprouts can be eaten when there is about 1cm (½in) of growth, or they can be left to grow for a day or two longer. When they are sprouted, leave the jar on a sunny window sill for about 3 hours – this will improve both their flavour and their nutrients. Then rinse and dry them well. They can be kept for about three days in the refrigerator.

## Cook's Tips
-------------------------------------------------

**Use only fresh bean sprouts**: when buying, look for plump, crisp white shoots; avoid those that feel limp or are starting to brown.

**Store bean sprouts** in a plastic bag in the refrigerator for up to two days.

**Rinse** in ice-cold water and drain well before use.

**2 3**

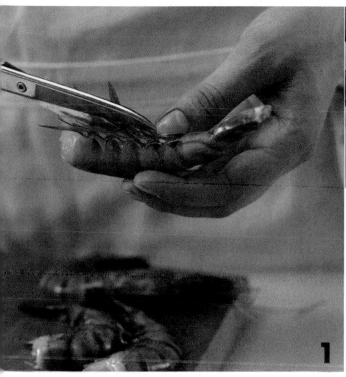

**1**

# Preparing shellfish

Always buy shellfish from a reputable fishmonger or a high-turnover fresh fish counter at a supermarket, and then prepare them within 24 hours. Most shellfish from supermarkets have previously been frozen, so don't re-freeze them.

## Prawns

Prawns are delicious stir-fried. They can be completely shelled, or you can leave the tail on, but they should be deveined before using.

**1** Pull off the head and discard (or put to one side and use later for making stock). Using pointed scissors, cut through the soft shell on the belly side.

**2** Prise the shell off, leaving the tail attached. (The shell can also be used later for making stock.)

**3** Using a small, sharp knife, make a shallow cut along the back of the prawn. Using the point of the knife, remove and discard the black vein (the intestinal tract) that runs along the back of the prawn.

## Mussels

Mussels take moments to cook, but careful preparation is important, so give yourself enough time to get the shellfish ready.

**1** Scrape off the fibres attached to the shells (beards). If the mussels are very clean, give them a quick rinse under the cold tap. If they are very sandy, scrub them with a stiff brush, then rinse thoroughly.

**2** If the shells have sizeable barnacles on them, it's best (though not essential) to remove them. Rap them sharply with a metal spoon or the back of a washing-up brush, then scrape off.

**3** Discard any open mussels that don't shut when sharply tapped; this means they are dead and may cause food poisoning.

**2 3**

**1**

## Ginger

**1** **Grating** Cut off a piece of the root and peel with a vegetable peeler. Cut off any brown spots.

**2** Rest the grater on a board or small plate and grate the ginger. Discard any large fibres adhering to the pulp.

**3** **Slicing, shredding and chopping** Cut slices off the ginger and cut off the skin carefully. Cut off any brown spots. Stack the slices and cut into shreds. To chop, stack the shreds and cut across into small pieces.

**4** **Pressing** If you just need the juice from the ginger, peel and cut off any brown spots, then cut into small chunks and use a garlic press held over a small bowl to extract the juice.

# Flavourings

Many stir-fry recipes begin by cooking garlic, ginger and spring onions as the basic flavourings. Spicier dishes may include chillies, lemongrass or a prepared spice paste such as Thai curry paste.

## Lemongrass

Lemongrass is a popular South East Asian ingredient, giving an aromatic, lemony flavour. It looks rather like a long, slender spring onion, but is fibrous and woody and is usually removed before the dish is served. Alternatively, the inner leaves may be very finely chopped or pounded in a mortar and pestle and used in spice pastes.

## Spring onions

Cut off the roots and trim any coarse or withered green parts. Slice diagonally, or shred by cutting into 5cm (2in) lengths and then slicing down the lengths, or chop finely, according to the recipe.

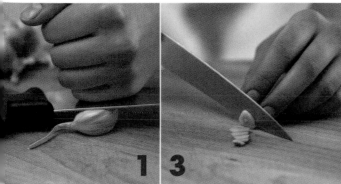

## Garlic

**1** Put the clove on a chopping board and place the flat side of a large knife on top of it. Press down firmly on the flat of the blade to crush the clove and break the papery skin.

**2** Cut off the base of the clove and slip the garlic out of its skin. It should come away easily.

**3** **Slicing** Using a rocking motion, with the knife tip on the board, slice the garlic as thinly as you need.

**4** **Shredding and chopping** Holding the slices together, shred them across the slices. Chop the shreds if you need chopped garlic.

**5** **Crushing** After step 2, the whole clove can be put into a garlic press. To crush with a knife: roughly chop the peeled cloves with a pinch of salt. Press down hard with the edge of a large knife (with the blade facing away from you), then drag the blade along the garlic while still pressing hard. Continue to do this, dragging the edge of the blade over the garlic.

## Cook's Tip

Wash hands thoroughly after handling chillies – the volatile oils will sting if accidentally rubbed into your eyes.

## Chillies

**1** Cut off the cap and then slit open lengthways. Using a spoon, scrape out the seeds and the pith.

**2** For diced chilli, cut into thin shreds lengthways, then cut crossways.

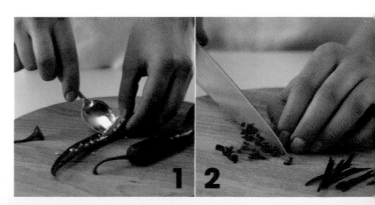

## Washing

**1** Trim the roots and part of the stalks from the herbs. Immerse in cold water and shake briskly. Leave in the water for a few minutes.

**2** Lift out of the water and put in a colander or sieve, then rinse again under the cold tap. Leave to drain for a few minutes, then dry thoroughly on kitchen paper or teatowels, or use a salad spinner.

# Using herbs

Most herbs are the leaf of a flowering plant and fresh herbs are usually sold with much of the stalk intact. They have to be washed, trimmed and then chopped or torn into pieces as suitable for your recipe.

## Chopping

**1** Trim the herbs by pinching off all but the smallest, most tender stalks. If the herb is one with a woody stalk, such as rosemary or thyme, it may be easier to remove the leaves by rubbing the whole bunch between your hands; the leaves should simply come off the stems.

**2** If you are chopping the leaves, gather them into a compact ball in one hand, keeping your fist around the ball (but being careful not to crush them).

**3** Chop with a large knife, using a rocking motion and letting just a little of the ball out of your fingers at a time.

**4** When the herbs are roughly chopped, continue chopping until the pieces are in small shreds or flakes.

# The Asian storecupboard

Rice and noodles (see page 14) are the staple foods of Asian cooking. The following items, used in many Asian dishes, are available in most large supermarkets and Asian food shops.

## Spices

**Chinese five-spice powder** is made from star anise, fennel seeds, cinnamon, cloves and Sichuan pepper. It has a strong, liquorice-like flavour and should be used sparingly.
**Kaffir lime leaves**, used in South East Asian cooking for their lime-lemon flavour, are glossy leaves used whole but not eaten – rather like bay leaves. Use grated lime zest as a substitute.
**Tamarind paste** has a delicately sour flavour; use lemon juice as a substitute.

## Sauces

**Black bean sauce** is made from fermented black beans, salt and ginger. Salty and pungent on its own, it adds richness to many stir-fry dishes.
**Chilli sauce** is made from fresh red chillies, vinegar, salt and sugar; some versions include other ingredients such as garlic or ginger. Sweet chilli sauce is a useful standby for adding piquancy to all kinds of dishes.
**Hoisin sauce**, sometimes called barbecue sauce, is a thick, sweet-spicy red-brown sauce.
**Oyster sauce** is a smooth brown sauce made from oyster extract, wheat flour and other flavourings. It doesn't taste fishy, but adds a 'meaty' flavour to stir-fries and braises.
**Plum sauce**, made from plums, ginger, chillies, vinegar and sugar, is traditionally served with duck or as a dip.
**Soy sauce** – made from fermented soya beans and, usually, wheat – is the most common flavouring in Chinese and South East Asian cooking. There are light and dark soy sauces; the dark kind is slightly sweeter and tends to darken the food. It will keep indefinitely.
**Thai fish sauce** is a salty condiment with a distinctive, pungent aroma. It is used in many South East Asian dishes. It will keep indefinitely.

**Thai green curry paste** is a blend of spices such as green chillies, coriander and lemongrass.
**Thai red curry paste** contains fresh and dried red chillies and ginger. Once opened, store in a sealed container in the refrigerator for up to one month.
**Yellow bean sauce** is a thick, salty, aromatic yellow-brown purée of fermented yellow soy beans, flour and salt.

## Canned vegetables

**Bamboo shoots**, available sliced or in chunks, have a mild flavour; rinse before use.
**Water chestnuts** have a very mild flavour but add a lovely crunch to stir-fried and braised dishes.

### Other ingredients

**Canned coconut milk** is widely available, but if you can't find it, use blocks of creamed coconut or coconut powder, following the packet instructions to make the amount of liquid you need.
**Dried mushrooms** feature in some Chinese recipes; they need to be soaked in hot water for 30 minutes before use.
**Dried shrimps and dried shrimp paste** (blachan) are often used in South East Asian cooking. The pungent smell becomes milder during cooking and the flavour marries with the other ingredients. These are often included in ready-made sauces and spice pastes, and are not suitable for vegetarians.
**Mirin** is a sweet rice wine from Japan; if you can't find it, use dry or medium sherry instead.
**Rice vinegar** is clear and milder than other vinegars. Use white wine vinegar or cider vinegar as a substitute.
**Rice wine** is often used in Chinese cooking; if you can't find it, use dry sherry instead.

## Which oil should I use?

**Groundnut (peanut) oil** has a mild flavour and is widely used in China and South East Asia. It is well suited to stir-frying and deep-frying as it has a high smoke point and can therefore be used at high temperatures. It usually has a bland flavour.
**Sesame oil** has a distinctive nutty flavour; it is best used in marinades or added as a seasoning to stir-fried dishes just before serving.
**Vegetable oil** may be pure rapeseed oil, or a blend of corn, soya bean, rapeseed or other oils.

# Making stock

Good stock can be the difference between a good dish and a great one. It gives depth of flavour to many dishes.

## Cook's Tips

To get a clearer liquid when making fish, meat or poultry stock, strain the cooked stock through four layers of muslin in a sieve.

**Stock** will keep for three days in the refrigerator.

**If you want to keep it** for a further three days, transfer it to a pan and re-boil gently for five minutes. Cool, put in a clean bowl and chill.

**When making meat or chicken stock**, make sure there is a good ratio of meat to bones. The more meat you use, the more flavour the stock will have.

# Stocks

## Vegetable Stock

**For 1.1 litres (2 pints), you will need:**
225g (8oz) each onions, celery, leeks and carrots, chopped, 2 bay leaves, a few thyme sprigs, 1 small bunch parsley, 10 black peppercorns, ½ tsp salt.

**1** Put all the ingredients in a pan and pour in 1.7 litres (3 pints) cold water.

**2** Bring slowly to the boil and skim the surface. Partially cover and simmer for 30 minutes. Adjust the seasoning. Strain the stock through a fine sieve into a bowl and leave to cool.

## Meat Stock

**For 900ml (1½ pints), you will need:**
450g (1lb) each meat bones and stewing meat, 1 onion, 2 celery sticks and 1 large carrot, sliced, 1 bouquet garni (2 bay leaves, a few thyme sprigs and a small bunch of parsley), 1 tsp black peppercorns, ½ tsp salt.

**1** Preheat the oven to 220°C (200°C fan oven) mark 7. Put the meat and bones in a roasting tin and roast for 30–40 minutes, turning now and again, until they are well browned.

**2** Put the bones and meat in a large pan with the remaining ingredients and add 2 litres (3½ pints) cold water. Bring slowly to the boil and skim the surface. Partially cover and simmer for 4–5 hours. Adjust the seasoning. Strain through a muslin-lined sieve into a bowl and cool quickly. Degrease (see opposite) before using.

## Chicken Stock

**For 1.1 litres (2 pints), you will need:**
1.6kg (3½lb) chicken bones, 225g (8oz) each onions and celery, sliced, 150g (5oz) chopped leeks, 1 bouquet garni (2 bay leaves, a few thyme sprigs and a small bunch parsley), 1 tsp black peppercorns, ½ tsp salt.

**1** Put all the ingredients in a large pan with 3 litres (5¼ pints) cold water.

**2** Bring slowly to the boil and skim the surface. Partially cover the pan and simmer gently for 2 hours. Adjust the seasoning if necessary.

**3** Strain the stock through a muslin-lined sieve into a bowl (see Cook's Tips) and cool quickly. Degrease (see right) before using.

## Fish Stock

**For 900ml (1½ pints), you will need:**
900g (2lb) fish bones and trimmings, washed, 2 carrots, 1 onion and 2 celery sticks, sliced, 1 bouquet garni (2 bay leaves, a few thyme sprigs and a small of bunch parsley), 6 white peppercorns, ½ tsp salt.

**1** Put all the ingredients in a large pan with 900ml (1½ pints) cold water.

**2** Bring slowly to the boil and skim the surface. Partially cover the pan and simmer gently for 30 minutes. Adjust the seasoning if necessary.

**3** Strain through a muslin-lined sieve into a bowl and cool quickly. Fish stock tends not to have much fat in it and so does not usually need to be degreased. However, if it does seem to be fatty, you will need to remove the fat by degreasing (see right).

# Degreasing stock

Meat and poultry stock needs to be degreased. (Vegetable stock does not.) You can mop the fat from the surface using kitchen paper, but the following methods are easier and more effective. There are three main methods that you can use: ladling, pouring and chilling.

**1** **Ladling** While the stock is warm, place a ladle on the surface. Press down to allow the fat floating on the surface to trickle over the edge until the ladle is full. Discard the fat, then repeat until all the fat has been removed.

**2** **Pouring** For this you need a degreasing jug or a double-pouring gravy boat, which has the spout at the base of the vessel. When you fill the jug or gravy boat with a fatty liquid, the fat rises. When you pour, the stock comes out while the fat stays behind in the jug.

**3** **Chilling** This technique works best with stock made from meat, whose fat solidifies when cold. Put the stock in the refrigerator until the fat becomes solid, then remove the pieces of fat using a slotted spoon.

## Hygiene

When you are preparing food, always follow these important guidelines:

**Wash your hands** thoroughly before handling food and again between handling different types of food, such as raw and cooked meat and poultry. If you have a graze or cut on your hand, cover it with a waterproof plaster.

**Wash down worksurfaces** regularly with a mild detergent solution or multi-surface cleaner.

**Use a dishwasher** if available. Otherwise, wear rubber gloves for washing-up, so that the water temperature can be hotter than unprotected hands can bear. Change drying-up cloths and cleaning cloths regularly. Note that leaving dishes to drain is more hygienic than drying them with a teatowel.

**Keep raw and cooked foods separate**, especially meat, fish and poultry. Wash kitchen utensils in between preparing raw and cooked foods. Never put cooked or ready-to-eat foods directly on to a surface that has just had raw fish, meat or poultry on it.

**Keep pets out of the kitchen** if possible and never allow animals on to worksurfaces.

# Food storage and hygiene

Storing food properly and preparing it in a hygienic way is important to ensure that food remains as nutritious and flavourful as possible, and to reduce the risk of food poisoning.

## Shopping

**Always choose fresh ingredients** in prime condition from stores and markets that have a regular turnover of stock, to ensure that you buy the freshest produce possible.

**Make sure items are within their 'best before' or 'use by' date.** (Foods with a long shelf life have a 'best before' date; more perishable items have a 'use by' date.)

**Pack frozen and chilled items** in an insulated cool bag at the check-out and put them into the freezer or refrigerator as soon as you get home.

**During warm weather** in particular, buy perishable foods just before you return home. When packing items at the check-out, sort them according to where you will store them when you get home – the refrigerator, freezer, storecupboard, vegetable rack, fruit bowl, etc. This will make unpacking easier – and quicker.

## The storecupboard

Although storecupboard ingredients will generally last a long time, correct storage is important:

**Always check packaging** for storage advice – even with familiar foods, because storage requirements may change if additives, sugar or salt have been reduced.

**Check storecupboard foods** for their 'best before' or 'use by' date and do not use them if the date has passed.

**Keep all food cupboards scrupulously clean** and make sure food containers and packets are properly sealed.

**Once opened, treat canned foods** as though fresh. Always transfer the contents to a clean container, cover and keep in the refrigerator. Similarly, jars, sauce bottles and cartons should be kept chilled after opening. (Check the label for safe storage times after opening.)

**Transfer dry goods** such as sugar, rice and pasta to moisture-proof containers. When supplies are used up, wash the container well and dry thoroughly before refilling with new supplies.

**Store oils** in a dark cupboard away from any heat source, as heat and light can make them turn rancid and affect their colour. For the same reason, buy olive oil in dark green bottles.

**Store vinegars** in a cool place; they can turn bad in a warm environment.

**Store dried herbs**, spices and flavourings in a cool, dark cupboard or in dark jars. Buy in small quantities as their flavour will not last indefinitely.

**Store flours and sugars** in airtight containers.

# Refrigerator storage

Fresh food needs to be kept in the cool temperature of the refrigerator to keep it in good condition and discourage the growth of harmful bacteria. Store day-to-day perishable items, such as opened jams and jellies, mayonnaise and bottled sauces, in the refrigerator along with eggs and dairy products, fruit juices, bacon, fresh and cooked meat (on separate shelves), and salads and vegetables (except potatoes, which don't suit being stored in the cold). A refrigerator should be kept at an operating temperature of 4–5°C.

**It is worth investing in a refrigerator thermometer** to check that the correct temperature is maintained. To ensure your refrigerator is functioning effectively for safe food storage, follow these guidelines:

**To avoid bacterial cross-contamination**, store cooked and raw foods on separate shelves, putting cooked foods on the top shelf. Ensure that all items are well wrapped.

**Never put hot food into the refrigerator**, as this will cause the internal temperature of the refrigerator to rise.

**Avoid overfilling the refrigerator**: it restricts the circulation of air and prevents the appliance from working properly.

**It can take some time** for the refrigerator to return to the correct operating temperature once the door has been opened, so don't leave it open any longer than is necessary.

**Clean the refrigerator regularly**, using a specially formulated germicidal refrigerator cleaner. Alternatively, use a weak solution of bicarbonate of soda: 1 tbsp to 1 litre (1¾ pints) water.

If your refrigerator doesn't have an automatic defrost facility, defrost regularly.

## Maximum refrigerator storage times

For pre-packed foods, always adhere to the 'use by' date on the packet. For other foods the following storage times should apply, providing the food is in prime condition when it goes into the refrigerator and that your refrigerator is in good working order.

### Vegetables
| | |
|---|---|
| Green vegetables | 3–4 days |
| Salad leaves | 2–3 days |

### Dairy food
| | |
|---|---|
| Cheese, hard | 1 week |
| Cheese, soft | 2–3 days |
| Eggs | 1 week |
| Milk | 4–5 days |

### Fish
| | |
|---|---|
| Fish | 1 day |
| Shellfish | 1 day |

### Raw meat
| | |
|---|---|
| Bacon | 7 days |
| Minced meat | 1 day |
| Poultry | 2 days |
| Raw sliced meat | 2 days |
| Sausages | 3 days |

### Cooked meat
| | |
|---|---|
| Sliced meat | 2 days |
| Ham | 2 days |
| Ham, vacuum-packed (or according to the instructions on the packet) | 1–2 weeks |

# 1

# Classic Dishes

## Cook's Tip

**Keep the oil from the anchovies** in the refrigerator for up to three days and use when frying onions, to give them added flavour.

# Spicy Tomato Pasta

300g (11oz) chunky pasta shapes

50g jar anchovies in oil with garlic and herbs

6 tomatoes, chopped

75g (3oz) pitted black olives, chopped

1 lemon, cut into wedges (if you like)

**1** Cook the pasta in a large pan of lightly salted boiling water according to the pack instructions.

**2** Drain the oil from the anchovies into a bowl and put 1 tbsp into a pan. Heat gently for 1 minute. Use the remaining oil for another recipe (see Cook's Tip).

**3** Add the anchovies to the hot oil and cook for 1 minute. Add the tomatoes and simmer for 10 minutes. Stir in the olives and cook for 1–2 minutes more.

**4** Drain the pasta, tip back into the pan and add the sauce. Toss together and serve with lemon wedges, if you like.

| Serves | EASY | | NUTRITIONAL INFORMATION | |
|---|---|---|---|---|
| 4 | **Preparation Time** 5 minutes | **Cooking Time** 15 minutes | **Per Serving** 343 calories, 7g fat (of which 1g saturates), 61g carbohydrate, 2g salt | Dairy free |

# Pasta Bake

2 tbsp vegetable oil
1 onion, finely chopped
2 garlic cloves, crushed
450g (1lb) extra-lean minced lamb
2 tbsp tomato purée
400g can chopped tomatoes
2 bay leaves
150ml (¼ pint) hot beef stock
350g (12oz) macaroni
50g (2oz) Cheddar cheese, grated
salt and ground black pepper

**For the sauce**

15g (½oz) butter
15g (½oz) plain flour
300ml (½ pint) milk
1 medium egg, beaten

**1** Heat the oil in a large pan, add the onion and garlic and cook for 5 minutes to soften. Add the lamb and stir-fry over a high heat for 3–4 minutes until browned all over.

**2** Add the tomato purée; cook for 1–2 minutes. Add the tomatoes, bay leaves and stock; season. Bring to the boil, reduce the heat and cook for 35–40 minutes.

**3** Meanwhile, make the sauce. Melt the butter in a pan, stir in the flour and cook over a medium heat for 1–2 minutes. Gradually add the milk, stirring constantly. Reduce the heat to low and cook, stirring, for 4–5 minutes. Remove from the heat; cool slightly. Stir in the beaten egg and season well. Put to one side.

**4** Preheat the oven to 180°C (160°C fan oven) mark 4. Cook the macaroni in a large pan of lightly salted boiling water, according to the pack instructions, until al dente.

**5** Drain the pasta well and spoon half into a 2 litre (3½ pint) ovenproof dish. Spoon the meat mixture over it, then top with the remaining macaroni. Pour the sauce evenly over the top and scatter with the grated cheese. Bake for 25–30 minutes until golden brown.

| EASY | | NUTRITIONAL INFORMATION | Serves |
|---|---|---|---|
| **Preparation Time** 10 minutes | **Cooking Time** About 1½ hours | **Per Serving** 736 calories, 30g fat (of which 13g saturates), 80g carbohydrate, 0.8g salt | **4** |

## Cook's Tip
-------------------------------------------------------------

**If using 'no need to pre-cook'** dried lasagne, add a little extra stock or water to the sauce.

# Classic Lasagne

1 quantity Bolognese Sauce (see page 13)

butter to grease

350g (12oz) fresh lasagne, or 225g (8oz) 'no need to pre-cook' dried lasagne (see Cook's Tip) (12–15 sheets)

1 quantity of Béchamel Sauce (see page 13)

3 tbsp freshly grated Parmesan

salad leaves to serve

**1** Preheat the oven to 180°C (160°C fan oven) mark 4. Spoon one-third of the Bolognese Sauce over the base of a greased 2.3 litre (4 pint) ovenproof dish. Cover with a layer of lasagne sheets, then a layer of béchamel sauce. Repeat these layers twice more, finishing with a layer of béchamel to cover the lasagne.

**2** Sprinkle the Parmesan over the top and stand the dish on a baking sheet. Cook in the oven for 45 minutes or until well browned and bubbling. Serve with salad leaves.

| Serves | EASY | | NUTRITIONAL INFORMATION |
|---|---|---|---|
| **6** | **Preparation Time** 40 minutes | **Cooking Time** 45 minutes (without the Bolognese Sauce) | **Per Serving** 367 calories, 14g fat (of which 5g saturates), 36g carbohydrate, 1.9g salt |

# Tagliatelle Carbonara

350g (12oz) tagliatelle

150g (5oz) smoked bacon, chopped

1 tbsp olive oil

2 large egg yolks

150ml (¼ pint) double cream

50g (2oz) freshly grated Parmesan

2 tbsp freshly chopped parsley

**1** Cook the pasta in a large pan of lightly salted boiling water according to the pack instructions. Drain.

**2** Meanwhile, fry the bacon in the oil for 4–5 minutes. Add to the drained pasta and keep hot.

**3** Put the egg yolks into a bowl, add the cream and whisk together. Add to the pasta with the Parmesan and parsley, toss well and serve.

| EASY | | NUTRITIONAL INFORMATION | Serves |
|---|---|---|---|
| **Preparation Time**<br>5 minutes | **Cooking Time**<br>10 minutes | **Per Serving**<br>688 calories, 39g fat (of which 19g saturates), 65g carbohydrate, 1.6g salt | **4** |

# Spaghetti Bolognese

500g (1lb 2oz) dried spaghetti
50g (2oz) Parmesan, freshly grated

**For the Bolognese sauce**
2 tbsp olive oil
1 onion, finely chopped
2 garlic cloves, crushed
450g (1lb) extra-lean minced beef
2 tbsp sun-dried tomato paste
300ml (½ pint) red wine
400g can chopped tomatoes
125g (4oz) chestnut mushrooms, sliced
2 tbsp Worcestershire sauce
salt and ground black pepper

**1** To make the Bolognese sauce, heat the olive oil in a large pan, add the onion and fry over a medium heat for 10 minutes or until softened and golden. Add the garlic and cook for 1 minute.

**2** Add the minced beef and brown evenly, using a wooden spoon to break up the pieces. Stir in the tomato paste and the red wine, cover and bring to the boil. Add the tomatoes, mushrooms and Worcestershire sauce, and season well with salt and pepper. Bring back to the boil, lower the heat and simmer for 20 minutes.

**3** Cook the spaghetti in a large pan of salted boiling water, according to the pack instructions, until al dente. Drain the pasta well, then return to the pan. Add the Bolognese sauce and toss to mix together. Check the seasoning.

**4** Divide among warmed plates and sprinkle with the Parmesan to serve.

## Try Something Different

Add 125g (4oz) chopped, rinded, smoked streaky bacon with the mince, brown, then stir in 200g (7oz) chopped chicken livers. Cook for 3 minutes before adding the tomato paste, then continue as above.

| Serves | EASY | | NUTRITIONAL INFORMATION |
|---|---|---|---|
| **6** | **Preparation Time** 15 minutes | **Cooking Time** 40 minutes | **Per Serving** 510 calories, 12g fat (of which 4g saturates), 67g carbohydrate, 1.5g salt |

# Macaroni Cheese

225g (8oz) short-cut macaroni

50g (2oz) butter

50g (2oz) plain flour

900ml (1½ pints) milk

½ tsp grated nutmeg or mustard powder

225g (8oz) mature Cheddar cheese, grated

3 tbsp fresh white or wholemeal breadcrumbs

salt and ground black pepper

**1** Cook the macaroni in a large pan of salted boiling water, according to the pack instructions, until al dente.

**2** Meanwhile, melt the butter in a pan, stir in the flour and cook, stirring, for 1 minute. Remove from the heat and gradually stir in the milk. Bring to the boil and cook, stirring, until the sauce thickens. Remove from the heat. Season with salt and pepper, and add the nutmeg or mustard.

**3** Drain the macaroni and add to the sauce, together with three-quarters of the cheese. Mix well, then turn into an ovenproof dish.

**4** Preheat the grill to high. Sprinkle the breadcrumbs and remaining cheese over the macaroni. Put under the grill for 2–3 minutes until golden brown on top and bubbling. Serve.

| Serves 4 | EASY | | NUTRITIONAL INFORMATION | |
|---|---|---|---|---|
| | **Preparation Time** 10 minutes | **Cooking Time** 15 minutes | **Per Serving** 680 calories, 34g fat (of which 21g saturates), 67g carbohydrate, 2g salt | Vegetarian |

## Cook's Tip

**Usually made from egg pasta,** cannelloni are large, broad tubes designed to be stuffed, coated in sauce and baked.

# Spinach and Ricotta Cannelloni

1 tbsp olive oil
1 small onion, chopped
1 bay leaf
1 garlic clove, crushed
400g can chopped tomatoes
300g (11oz) spinach, coarse stalks removed
2 × 250g tubs ricotta cheese
1 large egg
25g (1oz) freshly grated Parmesan
freshly grated nutmeg
15 cannelloni tubes
125g mozzarella ball, roughly pulled into small pieces
salt and ground black pepper
fresh basil leaves to garnish

**1** Heat the oil in a pan and gently fry the onion with the bay leaf for 10 minutes or until softened. Add the garlic and fry for 1 minute. Pour in the tomatoes along with half a can of cold water, bring to the boil, then simmer for 20 minutes or until slightly thickened.

**2** Meanwhile, wash the spinach and put into a large pan set over a low heat. Cover the pan and cook the spinach for 2 minutes or until just wilted. Drain and cool under running water. When cool enough to handle, squeeze out the excess moisture and chop roughly.

**3** Preheat the oven to 180°C (160°C fan oven) mark 4 and lightly oil a baking dish. Mix together the ricotta, egg, Parmesan and spinach with a grating of nutmeg and season with plenty of salt and ground black pepper. Spoon or pipe into the cannelloni tubes and put into the dish in one layer.

**4** Pour the tomato sauce over the pasta, then dot with the mozzarella. Bake for 30–40 minutes until golden and bubbling. Scatter with the basil and serve.

| EASY | | NUTRITIONAL INFORMATION | | Serves |
|---|---|---|---|---|
| **Preparation Time** 25 minutes | **Cooking Time** 1 hour 10 minutes | **Per Serving** 409 calories, 14g fat (of which 7g saturates), 53g carbohydrate, 1.5g salt | Vegetarian | **4** |

### Cook's Tip

--------------------------------------------------------

**Use an oil-water spray for frying,** as it will add far fewer calories than oil alone and, as it sprays on thinly and evenly, you'll use less. Fill one-eighth of a travel-sized spray bottle with oil such as sunflower, light olive or vegetable (rapeseed) oil, then top up with water.
To use, shake well before spraying.
Store in the fridge.

# Italian Meatballs

50g (2oz) fresh breadcrumbs
450g (1lb) minced lean pork
1 tsp fennel seeds, crushed, plus ¼ tsp chilli flakes
3 garlic cloves, crushed
4 tbsp freshly chopped flat-leafed parsley
3 tbsp red wine
spaghetti to serve

**For the tomato sauce**
oil-water spray
2 large shallots, finely chopped
3 pitted black olives, shredded
2 garlic cloves, crushed
2 pinches of chilli flakes
250ml (9fl oz) vegetable or chicken stock
500g carton passata
2 tbsp each freshly chopped flat-leafed parsley, basil and oregano, plus oregano to garnish
salt and ground black pepper

**1** To make the tomato sauce, spray a pan with the oil-water spray and add the shallots. Cook gently for 5 minutes. Add the olives, garlic, chilli flakes and stock and bring to the boil, then reduce the heat, cover and simmer for 3–4 minutes.

**2** Uncover and simmer for 10 minutes, or until the shallots and garlic are soft and the liquid syrupy. Stir in the passata and season with salt and pepper. Bring to the boil, then reduce the heat and simmer for 10–15 minutes. Stir in the herbs.

**3** Meanwhile, put the breadcrumbs, pork, fennel seeds, chilli flakes, garlic, parsley and wine into a large bowl, season and mix together, using your hands, until thoroughly combined. (To check the seasoning, fry a little mixture, taste and adjust if necessary.)

**4** With wet hands, roll the mixture into balls. Line a grill pan with foil, shiny-side upwards, and spray with the oil-water spray. Cook the meatballs under a preheated grill for 3–4 minutes on each side. Serve with the tomato sauce and spaghetti, garnished with oregano.

| Serves 4 | EASY | | NUTRITIONAL INFORMATION | |
|---|---|---|---|---|
| | **Preparation Time** 15 minutes | **Cooking Time** 50 minutes | **Per Serving** 275 calories, 12g fat (of which 4g saturates), 16g carbohydrate, 1.8g salt | Dairy free |

# Chicken Chow Mein

250g (9oz) medium egg noodles

1 tbsp toasted sesame oil

2 boneless, skinless chicken breasts, about 125g (4oz) each, cut into thin strips

1 bunch of spring onions, thinly sliced diagonally

150g (5oz) mangetouts, thickly sliced diagonally

125g (4oz) bean sprouts

100g (3½oz) cooked ham, finely shredded

120g sachet chow mein sauce

salt and ground black pepper

light soy sauce to serve

**1** Cook the noodles in boiling water for 4 minutes or according to the pack instructions. Drain, rinse thoroughly in cold water, drain again and put to one side.

**2** Meanwhile, heat a wok or large frying pan until hot, then add the oil. Add the chicken and stir-fry over a high heat for 3–4 minutes until browned all over. Add the spring onions and mangetouts and stir-fry for 2 minutes. Stir in the bean sprouts and ham and cook for a further 2 minutes.

**3** Add the drained noodles, then pour in the chow mein sauce and toss together to coat evenly. Stir-fry for 2 minutes or until piping hot. Season with salt and pepper and serve immediately, with light soy sauce to drizzle over the chow mein.

| EASY | | NUTRITIONAL INFORMATION | Serves |
|---|---|---|---|
| **Preparation Time** 10 minutes | **Cooking Time** 10 minutes | **Per Serving** 451 calories, 11g fat (of which 2g saturates), 59g carbohydrate, 1.3g salt | 4 |

# Quick Pad Thai

250g (9oz) wide ribbon rice noodles

3 tbsp satay and sweet chilli pesto (see Cook's Tips)

125g (4oz) mangetouts, thinly sliced

125g (4oz) sugarsnap peas, thinly sliced

3 medium eggs, beaten

3 tbsp chilli soy sauce, plus extra to serve (see Cook's Tips)

250g (9oz) cooked and peeled tiger prawns

25g (1oz) dry-roasted peanuts, roughly crushed

lime wedges to serve (optional)

**1** Put the noodles into a heatproof bowl, cover with boiling water and soak for 4 minutes until softened. Drain, rinse under cold water and put aside.

**2** Heat a wok or large frying pan until hot, add the chilli pesto and stir-fry for 1 minute. Add the mangetouts and sugarsnap peas and cook for a further 2 minutes. Tip into a bowl. Put the pan back on the heat, add the eggs and cook, stirring, for 1 minute.

**3** Add the soy sauce, prawns and noodles to the pan. Toss well and cook for 3 minutes or until piping hot. Return the vegetables to the pan and cook for a further 1 minute until heated through, then sprinkle with the peanuts. Serve with extra soy sauce, and lime wedges to squeeze over the Pad Thai, if you like.

## Cook's Tips
-----------------------------------------------------

**If you can't find satay and sweet chilli pesto,** substitute 2 tbsp peanut butter and 1 tbsp sweet chilli sauce.
**Chilli soy sauce** can be replaced with 2 tbsp light soy sauce and ½ red chilli, finely chopped (see Cook's Tip, page 23).

| EASY | | NUTRITIONAL INFORMATION | | Serves |
|---|---|---|---|---|
| **Preparation Time** 12 minutes, plus soaking | **Cooking Time** 8 minutes | **Per Serving** 451 calories, 13g fat (of which 3g saturates), 56g carbohydrate, 2.6g salt | Dairy free | **4** |

1 lemongrass stalk, inner leaves only, finely chopped

100g (3½oz) medium egg noodles

100g (3½oz) sugarsnap peas, halved diagonally

4 tbsp vegetable oil

4 garlic cloves, crushed

3 large eggs, beaten

juice of 2 lemons

3 tbsp Thai fish sauce

2 tbsp light soy sauce

½ tsp caster sugar

50g (2oz) roasted salted peanuts

½ tsp chilli powder

12 spring onions, roughly chopped

150g (5oz) bean sprouts

2 tbsp freshly chopped coriander, plus extra to garnish

salt and ground black pepper

# Thai Egg Noodles

**1** Put the lemongrass into a heatproof bowl with the noodles. Pour in 600ml (1 pint) boiling water and put to one side for 20 minutes, stirring from time to time.

**2** Cook the sugarsnap peas in lightly salted boiling water for 1 minute, then drain and plunge them into ice-cold water.

**3** Heat the oil in a wok or large frying pan, add the garlic and fry for 30 seconds. Add the beaten eggs and cook gently until lightly scrambled. Add the lemon juice, fish sauce, soy sauce, sugar, peanuts, chilli powder, spring onions and bean sprouts to the eggs. Pour the noodles, lemongrass and soaking liquid into the pan. Bring to the boil and bubble for 4–5 minutes, stirring from time to time.

**4** Drain the sugarsnap peas, then add them to the noodle mixture with the chopped coriander. Heat through and season with salt and pepper. Garnish with coriander and serve immediately.

| Serves | EASY | | NUTRITIONAL INFORMATION | |
|---|---|---|---|---|
| 4 | **Preparation Time** 15 minutes | **Cooking Time** 12–15 minutes | **Per Serving** 289 calories, 18g fat (of which 3g saturates), 24g carbohydrate, 2.9g salt | Dairy free |

## Try Something Different

**Instead of prawns,** try chicken cut into strips; stir-fry for 5 minutes in step 1. Or, instead of raw prawns, use frozen cooked prawns.

# Quick Stir-fry

1 tbsp sesame oil

175g (6oz) raw peeled prawns, deveined (see page 21)

50ml (2fl oz) ready-made sweet chilli and ginger sauce

225g (8oz) stir-fry vegetables, such as sliced courgettes, broccoli and green beans

**1** Heat the oil in a large wok or frying pan, add the prawns and sweet chilli and ginger sauce, and stir-fry for 2 minutes.

**2** Add the mixed vegetables and stir-fry for a further 2–3 minutes until the prawns are cooked and the vegetables are heated through. Serve immediately.

| EASY | | NUTRITIONAL INFORMATION | | Serves |
|---|---|---|---|---|
| **Preparation Time** 4 minutes | **Cooking Time** 5 minutes | **Per Serving** 170 calories, 7g fat (of which 1g saturates), 11g carbohydrate, 1.6g salt | Gluten free Dairy free | 2 |

# 2

# Fish and Shellfish

# Pasta with Anchovies, Tomatoes and Olives

50g can anchovy fillets in oil

2 garlic cloves, crushed

4 sun-dried tomatoes, drained and roughly chopped

400g can chopped tomatoes

500g (1lb 2oz) dried spaghetti

200g (7oz) pitted black olives, roughly chopped

2 tbsp capers, drained

2–3 tbsp freshly chopped flat-leafed parsley

salt and ground black pepper

**1** Drain the oil from the anchovies into a large pan. Heat the oil, then add the garlic and cook for 1 minute. Add the anchovies and sun-dried tomatoes and cook, stirring, for a further 1 minute. Add the canned tomatoes and bring to the boil. Season well with salt and pepper and simmer for 10–15 minutes.

**2** Meanwhile, cook the spaghetti in a large pan of salted boiling water, according to the pack instructions, until al dente.

**3** Stir the olives and capers into the tomato sauce. Drain the spaghetti thoroughly, reserving about 4 tbsp of the cooking water, then return to the pan.

**4** Add the tomato sauce and chopped parsley to the pasta and toss well to mix, thinning the sauce with the reserved cooking water, if necessary. Serve at once.

| Serves | EASY | | NUTRITIONAL INFORMATION |
|--------|------|------|-------------------------|
| **4** | **Preparation Time** 15 minutes | **Cooking Time** 20–25 minutes | **Per Serving** 620 calories, 12g fat (of which 2g saturates), 96g carbohydrate, 4.5g salt |

# Kale, Anchovy and Crispy Breadcrumb Pasta

75g (3oz) fresh breadcrumbs

300g (11oz) orecchiette or other shaped pasta

150g (5oz) kale, shredded

2 tbsp olive oil

1 red chilli, seeded and finely chopped (see page 23)

100g jar anchovies, drained and chopped

25g (1oz) Parmesan, freshly grated

**1** Preheat the grill to medium and toast the breadcrumbs.

**2** Cook the pasta according to the pack instructions until al dente. Add the kale to the pasta for the last 5–6 minutes of cooking time.

**3** Heat 1 tbsp oil in a pan and fry the chilli and anchovies for 3–4 minutes.

**4** Drain the pasta and kale, then tip back into the pan. Add the breadcrumbs, the anchovy mixture, the remaining oil and the Parmesan. Toss to mix, then serve.

| EASY | | NUTRITIONAL INFORMATION | Serves |
|---|---|---|---|
| **Preparation Time**<br>5 minutes | **Cooking Time**<br>15 minutes | **Per Serving**<br>481 calories, 14g fat (of which 2g saturates), 72g carbohydrate, 3g salt | **4** |

225g can tuna steak in olive oil

1 onion, finely sliced

1 garlic clove, chopped

2 × 400g cans chopped tomatoes

500g (1lb 2oz) dried penne or other pasta

50g can anchovy fillets in oil, drained and chopped

2 tbsp small capers

2 tbsp basil leaves, roughly torn (optional)

salt and ground black pepper

# Tuna Pasta

**1** Drain the oil from the tuna into a pan and put the tuna to one side.

**2** Heat the tuna oil, then add the sliced onion and fry over a low heat for 10 minutes or until softened but not browned. Add the chopped garlic and cook for 1 minute.

**3** Add the tomatoes and stir well. Season generously with salt and pepper, then simmer over a medium heat for 15 minutes to reduce and thicken the sauce.

**4** Meanwhile, cook the pasta in a large pan of salted boiling water, according to the pack instructions, until al dente.

**5** Flake the tuna and add to the tomato sauce with the anchovies, capers and basil leaves, if using. Stir to mix well.

**6** Drain the pasta well, return to the pan and add the tuna sauce. Toss everything together to mix and serve immediately in warmed bowls.

| Serves | EASY | | NUTRITIONAL INFORMATION |
|---|---|---|---|
| 4 | **Preparation Time** 10 minutes | **Cooking Time** 30 minutes | **Per Serving** 650 calories, 16g fat (of which 2g saturates), 102g carbohydrate, 2.3g salt |

## Cook's Tip

**Adding the reserved** pasta cooking water stops the pasta absorbing too much of the crème fraîche.

# Simple Salmon Pasta

500g (1lb 2oz) dried linguine pasta
a little olive oil
1 fat garlic clove, crushed
200ml (7fl oz) half-fat crème fraîche
225g (8oz) hot-smoked salmon, flaked
200g (7oz) peas
basil leaves to garnish
salt and ground black pepper

**1** Cook the pasta according to the pack instructions, then drain, reserving a couple of tablespoons of the cooking water.

**2** Meanwhile, heat the oil in a large pan, add the garlic and fry gently until golden. Add the crème fraîche, the flaked salmon and peas, and stir in. Cook for 1–2 minutes until warmed through, then add the reserved water from the pasta.

**3** Toss the pasta in the sauce, season with salt and pepper and serve immediately, garnished with basil.

| EASY | | NUTRITIONAL INFORMATION | Serves |
|---|---|---|---|
| **Preparation Time** 2 minutes | **Cooking Time** 10 minutes | **Per Serving** 630 calories, 13g fat (of which 6g saturates), 100g carbohydrate, 2.7g salt | **4** |

# Penne with Smoked Salmon

350g (12oz) penne or other short tubular pasta
200ml (7fl oz) half-fat crème fraîche
150g (5oz) smoked salmon, roughly chopped
20g (¾ oz) fresh dill, finely chopped
salt and ground black pepper
lemon wedges to serve (optional)

**1** Cook the pasta in a large pan of lightly salted boiling water, according to the pack instructions, until al dente. Drain.

**2** Meanwhile, put the crème fraîche into a large bowl. Add the smoked salmon and chopped dill, season well with salt and pepper and mix together. Gently stir into the drained penne and serve immediately with lemon wedges, if you like, to squeeze over the salmon and pasta.

| Serves | EASY | | NUTRITIONAL INFORMATION |
|---|---|---|---|
| 4 | **Preparation Time** 5 minutes | **Cooking Time** 10–15 minutes | **Per Serving** 432 calories, 11g fat (of which 6g saturates), 67g carbohydrate, 1.7g salt |

300g (11oz) linguine pasta

2 tbsp olive oil

1 garlic clove, crushed

1 red chilli, seeded and finely chopped (see page 23)

4 tomatoes, seeded and chopped

900g (2lb) clams in their shells, washed and scrubbed

150ml (¼ pint) light dry white wine

2 tbsp freshly chopped parsley

# Clams with Chilli Linguine

**1** Cook the linguine according to the pack instructions.

**2** Meanwhile, heat the oil in a large pan. Add the garlic, chilli and tomatoes and fry for 4 minutes, stirring gently. Add the clams and wine. Cover the pan with a lid and cook over a high heat for 3–4 minutes until the clam shells spring open – discard any that remain closed.

**3** Drain the pasta, return to the pan, then add the clams with the sauce and the parsley. Toss together gently and serve immediately.

| EASY | | NUTRITIONAL INFORMATION | | Serves |
|---|---|---|---|---|
| **Preparation Time** 15 minutes | **Cooking Time** About 10 minutes | **Per Serving** 405 calories, 8g fat (of which 1g saturates), 60g carbohydrate, 2.3g salt | Dairy free | **4** |

# Spaghetti with Mussels

1kg (2lb) fresh mussels in their shells, cleaned (see page 21)

1kg (2lb) ripe, flavourful tomatoes, quartered

1 onion, chopped

4 garlic cloves

6 basil leaves, plus extra to garnish

150ml (½ pint) white wine

400g (14oz) dried spaghetti

2 tbsp olive oil

2 red chillies, halved, seeded and chopped (see page 23)

salt and ground black pepper

**1** Put the mussels into a large pan with a cupful of water. Cover with a tight-fitting lid and cook for 3–4 minutes, shaking the pan occasionally, until the mussels open. Using a slotted spoon, transfer the mussels to a bowl and discard any unopened ones.

**2** Strain the mussel cooking juices through a muslin-lined sieve and set aside.

**3** Put the tomatoes and onion into a shallow pan. Crush 2 garlic cloves and add them to the pan with the basil. Bring to the boil, then lower the heat and simmer for about 20 minutes until the tomatoes begin to disintegrate.

**4** Press through a nylon sieve or mouli-légumes into a clean pan. Pour in the reserved mussel liquid and the wine. Bring to the boil and let bubble until reduced by half.

**5** Cook the spaghetti according to the pack instructions until al dente.

**6** Meanwhile, heat the oil in another pan. Chop the remaining garlic and add to the pan with the chillies. Cook until golden, then stir in the tomato sauce and mussels. Cover and simmer for 2–3 minutes until heated through. Season with salt and pepper to taste.

**7** Drain the spaghetti, keeping 2 tbsp of the cooking water. Toss the spaghetti and reserved water with the mussel sauce. Serve immediately, garnished with basil.

| Serves 4 | EASY | | NUTRITIONAL INFORMATION | |
|---|---|---|---|---|
| | **Preparation Time** 20 minutes | **Cooking Time** 35 minutes | **Per Serving** 530 calories, 10g fat (of which 1.5g saturates), 83g carbohydrate, 0.5g salt | Dairy free |

# Seafood Spaghetti with Pepper and Almond Sauce

1 small red pepper

1 red chilli (see page 23)

50g (2oz) blanched almonds

2–3 garlic cloves, chopped

2 tbsp red wine vinegar

350ml (12fl oz) tomato juice

a small handful of flat-leafed parsley

300g (11oz) spaghetti

450g (1lb) mixed cooked seafood, such as prawns, mussels and squid

salt and ground black pepper

**1** Preheat the grill. Grill the red pepper and chilli, turning occasionally, until the skins char and blacken. Cover and leave to cool slightly, then peel off the skins. Halve, discard the seeds, then put the flesh into a food processor.

**2** Toast the almonds under the grill until golden. Add the toasted almonds and garlic to the processor with the vinegar, tomato juice and half the parsley, then season with salt and pepper. Whizz until almost smooth, then transfer the sauce to a large pan.

**3** Meanwhile, cook the spaghetti in a pan of lightly salted boiling water according to the pack instructions; keep it al dente.

**4** Heat the sauce gently until it simmers, then add the seafood. Simmer for 3–4 minutes until the sauce and seafood are heated through, stirring frequently.

**5** Roughly chop the remaining parsley. Drain the pasta and return to the pan, then add the sauce together with the parsley and toss well.

| Serves 4 | EASY | | NUTRITIONAL INFORMATION | |
|---|---|---|---|---|
| | **Preparation Time** 20 minutes | **Cooking Time** 25 minutes | **Per Serving** 426 calories, 9g fat (of which 1g saturates), 62g carbohydrate, 0.9g salt | Dairy free |

# Stir-fried Salmon and Broccoli

2 tsp sesame oil

1 red pepper, seeded and thinly sliced

½ red chilli, seeded and thinly sliced (see page 23)

1 garlic clove, crushed

125g (4oz) broccoli florets

2 spring onions, sliced

2 salmon fillets, about 125g (4oz) each, cut into strips

1 tsp Thai fish sauce

2 tsp soy sauce

wholewheat noodles to serve

**1** Heat the oil in a wok or large frying pan. Add the red pepper, chilli, garlic, broccoli and spring onions and stir-fry over a high heat for 3–4 minutes.

**2** Add the salmon, fish sauce and soy sauce and cook for 2 minutes, stirring gently. Serve immediately with wholewheat noodles.

| EASY | | NUTRITIONAL INFORMATION | | Serves |
|---|---|---|---|---|
| **Preparation Time** 10 minutes | **Cooking Time** 5–6 minutes | **Per Serving** 90 calories, 4g fat (of which 1g saturates), 9g carbohydrate, 2.7g salt | Dairy free | **2** |

## Cook's Tip

--------------------------------------------------------

**Don't overcook** this dish or the noodles will be soggy and
the prawns tough.

# Thai Noodles with Prawns

4–6 tsp Thai red curry paste

175g (6oz) medium egg noodles (wholewheat if possible)

2 small red onions, chopped

1 lemongrass stalk, trimmed and sliced

1 fresh red bird's-eye chilli, seeded and finely chopped
(see page 23)

300ml (½ pint) reduced-fat coconut milk

400g (14oz) raw tiger prawns, peeled and deveined (see
page 21)

4 tbsp freshly chopped coriander, plus extra freshly torn
coriander to garnish

salt and ground black pepper

**1** Pour 2 litres (3½ pints) water into a large pan and
bring to the boil. Add the curry paste, noodles,
onions, lemongrass, chilli and coconut milk and bring
back to the boil.

**2** Add the prawns and chopped coriander, reduce the
heat and simmer for 2–3 minutes until the prawns
turn pink. Season with salt and pepper.

**3** Divide the prawns and noodles among four large
bowls and sprinkle with the torn coriander.

| Serves 4 | EASY | | NUTRITIONAL INFORMATION | |
|---|---|---|---|---|
| | **Preparation Time** 10 minutes | **Cooking Time** 5 minutes | **Per Serving** 343 calories, 11g fat (of which 2g saturates), 40g carbohydrate, 1g salt | Dairy free |

## Cook's Tip

**Ready-prepared stir-fry vegetables** make this an extra-quick dish, but if you can't find them, try a mixture of three or four of the following: strips of red, orange or yellow peppers, baby sweetcorn, mangetouts or sugarsnaps, carrots cut into matchsticks, or bean sprouts.

# Prawn and Peanut Noodles

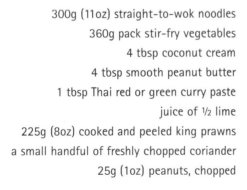

300g (11oz) straight-to-wok noodles
360g pack stir-fry vegetables
4 tbsp coconut cream
4 tbsp smooth peanut butter
1 tbsp Thai red or green curry paste
juice of ½ lime
225g (8oz) cooked and peeled king prawns
a small handful of freshly chopped coriander
25g (1oz) peanuts, chopped

**1** Put the noodles and stir-fry vegetables into a large bowl or wok and cover with boiling water. Cover with clingfilm and leave for 5 minutes.

**2** Meanwhile, mix the coconut cream with the peanut butter, curry paste and lime juice in a bowl.

**3** Drain the noodles and vegetables in a colander. Put back into the bowl and toss with the prawns, coriander and half the dressing. Sprinkle with the peanuts and serve with the remaining dressing.

| EASY | | NUTRITIONAL INFORMATION | | Serves |
|---|---|---|---|---|
| **Preparation Time** 10 minutes | **Cooking Time** 5 minutes' soaking | **Per Serving** 579 calories, 24g fat (of which 7g saturates), 67g carbohydrate, 0.7g salt | Vegetarian Dairy free | 4 |

**Try Something Different**

- - - - - - - - - - - - - - - - - - - - - - - - - - - - - - - - - -

**Use chicken**, cut into thin strips, instead of the prawns.

# Yellow Bean Noodles with Tiger Prawns

250g (9oz) medium egg noodles

1 tbsp stir-fry oil or sesame oil

1 garlic clove, sliced

1 tsp freshly grated root ginger

1 bunch of spring onions, each cut into four

250g (9oz) raw peeled tiger prawns (see page 21), thawed if frozen

200g (7oz) pak choi, leaves separated and white base cut into thick slices

160g jar Chinese yellow bean stir-fry sauce

**1** Put the noodles in a large heatproof bowl and pour 2 litres (3½ pints) boiling water over them. Leave to soak for 4 minutes. Drain and set aside.

**2** Heat the oil in a wok or large frying pan. Add the garlic and ginger, then stir-fry for 30 seconds. Add the spring onions and prawns and cook for 2 minutes.

**3** Boil the kettle. Add the sliced white pak choi stems to the pan with the yellow bean sauce. Fill the sauce jar with boiling water, pour it into the pan and stir well to mix.

**4** Add the drained noodles to the pan and cook for 1 minute, tossing every now and then, until heated through. Stir in the pak choi leaves and serve immediately.

| Serves | EASY | | NUTRITIONAL INFORMATION | |
|---|---|---|---|---|
| **4** | **Preparation Time**<br>10 minutes, plus<br>4 minutes' soaking | **Cooking Time**<br>5 minutes | **Per Serving**<br>403 calories, 10g fat (of which 2g saturates),<br>62g carbohydrate, 0.7g salt | Dairy free |

## Cook's Tips

**Tamari** is a wheat-free Japanese soy sauce.
**Soba noodles** are made from buckwheat and are gluten free. If you have a wheat allergy or gluten intolerance, check that the pack specifies '100 per cent soba'.
**Furikake seasoning** is a Japanese condiment consisting of sesame seeds and chopped dried seaweed; it can be found in supermarkets and Asian food shops.

550g (1¼lb) salmon fillet, cut into 1cm (½in) slices

3 tbsp teriyaki sauce

3 tbsp tamari (see Cook's Tips) or light soy sauce

2 tbsp vegetable oil

1 tbsp sesame oil

1 tbsp freshly chopped chives

2 tsp peeled and grated fresh root ginger

2 garlic cloves, crushed

350g (12oz) soba noodles (see Cook's Tips)

350g (12oz) baby spinach leaves

furikake seasoning (see Cook's Tips)

# Teriyaki Salmon with Spinach

**1** Gently mix the salmon slices with the teriyaki sauce, then cover, chill and leave to marinate for 1 hour.

**2** Mix together the tamari or soy sauce, 1 tbsp vegetable oil, the sesame oil, chives, ginger and garlic. Put to one side.

**3** Cook the noodles in boiling water according to the pack instructions. Drain and put to one side.

**4** Heat the remaining vegetable oil in a wok or large frying pan. Remove the salmon from the marinade and add it to the pan. Cook over a high heat until it turns opaque – about 30 seconds. Remove from the pan and put to one side.

**5** Add the drained noodles to the pan and stir until warmed through. Stir in the spinach and cook for 1–2 minutes until the leaves have wilted. Add the soy sauce mixture and stir to combine. Divide the noodles among four deep bowls, then top with the salmon. Sprinkle with furikake seasoning and serve.

| EASY | | NUTRITIONAL INFORMATION | | Serves |
|---|---|---|---|---|
| **Preparation Time** 10 minutes, plus marinating | **Cooking Time** 6 minutes | **Per Serving** 672 calories, 30g fat (of which 4g saturates), 66g carbohydrate, 2.9g salt | Dairy free | **4** |

# Mee Goreng

125g (4oz) rump steak, very thinly sliced across the grain

2 garlic cloves

2 tbsp soy sauce

450g (1lb) cleaned squid

225g (8oz) egg noodles

1 tbsp vegetable oil

1 tbsp sesame oil

1–2 hot red chillies, chopped (see page 23)

2.5cm (1in) piece fresh root ginger, peeled and finely chopped

2–3 spring onions, sliced

175g (6oz) large raw peeled prawns, deveined (see page 21)

2 tbsp hoisin sauce

1 tbsp lemon juice

2 tbsp Thai fish sauce

125g (4oz) bean sprouts

1 medium egg, beaten

lemon wedges to serve

**1** Put the steak in a shallow dish with 1 garlic clove and 1 tbsp soy sauce. Leave to stand.

**2** Wash and dry the squid. Cut the tentacles into small pieces. Open out the body pouches and cut into small rectangular pieces.

**3** Put the noodles in a large heatproof bowl and pour plenty of boiling water over them. Leave to soak for about 4 minutes or according to the pack instructions.

**4** Heat the vegetable and sesame oils in a wok or large frying pan, add the remaining garlic, the chillies, ginger and spring onions and cook for 2 minutes, stirring all the time.

**5** Add the beef and cook for 2 minutes. Add the squid and prawns and cook for 2 minutes. Add the hoisin sauce, lemon juice, fish sauce and remaining soy sauce and cook for 2 minutes.

**6** Drain the noodles and add them to the pan with the bean sprouts. Cook for a couple of minutes until heated through, then add the beaten egg. Cook briefly until the egg is on the point of setting. Serve immediately, with lemon wedges to squeeze over it.

## Try Something Different

**For a less elaborate** version of this Malaysian dish, omit the squid and replace the raw prawns with 225g (8oz) cooked peeled prawns.

| A LITTLE EFFORT | | NUTRITIONAL INFORMATION | | Serves |
|---|---|---|---|---|
| **Preparation Time** 30 minutes | **Cooking Time** About 12 minutes | **Per Serving** 306 calories, 11g fat (of which 3g saturates), 31g carbohydrate, 2g salt | Dairy free | **6** |

# 3

# Chicken and Poultry

# Pasta with Chicken, Cream and Basil

1 tbsp olive oil

2 shallots, chopped

400g (14oz) boneless chicken, cubed

125g (4oz) chestnut mushrooms, sliced

50g (2oz) sultanas

a pinch of ground cinnamon

50ml (2fl oz) dry white wine

125ml (4fl oz) hot chicken stock

300g (11oz) farfalle pasta

142ml carton double cream

2 tsp Dijon mustard

2 tsp freshly chopped basil

salt

**1** Heat the oil in a pan. Add the shallots and fry for 4–5 minutes. Add the chicken and cook until browned. Add the mushrooms and cook for 2 minutes. Stir in the sultanas and cinnamon.

**2** Pour in the wine and hot stock and simmer for 12–15 minutes until the chicken is cooked.

**3** Meanwhile, cook the pasta in a large pan of lightly salted boiling water according to the pack instructions.

**4** Stir the cream, mustard and basil into the chicken and season with salt. Drain the pasta and return to the pan, then add the sauce, toss and serve.

| Serves 4 | EASY | | NUTRITIONAL INFORMATION |
| --- | --- | --- | --- |
| | **Preparation Time** 10 minutes | **Cooking Time** 25 minutes | **Per Serving** 612 calories, 27g fat (of which 12g saturates), 67g carbohydrate, 0.4g salt |

**Try Something Different**

----------------------------------------------------

**Instead of boneless chicken thighs,** buy thighs on the bone and cut the meat off. This is a cheaper option.

# Chicken, Bacon and Leek Pasta Bake

1 tbsp olive oil

100g (3½oz) chopped streaky bacon rashers

450g (1lb) boneless, skinless chicken thighs, chopped

3 medium leeks, trimmed and chopped

300g (11oz) macaroni or other pasta shapes

350g carton ready-made cheese sauce

2 tsp Dijon mustard

2 tbsp freshly chopped flat-leafed parsley

25g (1oz) freshly grated Parmesan

**1** Heat the oil in a large frying pan. Add the bacon and chicken and cook for 7–8 minutes. Add the leeks and continue cooking for 4–5 minutes.

**2** Meanwhile, cook the pasta in a large pan of lightly salted boiling water according to the pack instructions. Drain well.

**3** Preheat the grill. Add the cheese sauce to the pasta with the mustard, chicken mixture and parsley. Mix well, then tip into a 2.1 litre (3¾ pint) ovenproof dish and sprinkle with Parmesan. Grill for 4–5 minutes until golden.

| EASY | | NUTRITIONAL INFORMATION | Serves |
|---|---|---|---|
| **Preparation Time** 10 minutes | **Cooking Time** 20 minutes | **Per Serving** 650 calories, 24g fat (of which 6g saturates), 68g carbohydrate, 2.2g salt | **4** |

# Chilli-fried Chicken with Coconut Noodles

2 tbsp plain flour

1 tsp mild chilli powder

1 tsp ground ginger

½ tsp salt

1 tsp caster sugar

6 boneless, skinless chicken breasts, about 150g (5oz) each, cut diagonally into three

250g (9oz) thread egg noodles

3 tbsp groundnut oil

1 large bunch of spring onions, sliced

1½ tsp Thai red curry paste or tandoori paste

150g (5oz) salted roasted peanuts, finely chopped

6 tbsp coconut milk

**1** Mix the flour, chilli powder, ground ginger, salt and sugar in a bowl. Dip the chicken into the spiced flour and coat well.

**2** Cook the noodles in boiling water according to the pack instructions, then drain.

**3** Heat the oil in a frying pan. Add the chicken and fry for 5 minutes or until cooked. Put to one side, cover and keep warm.  Add the spring onions to the pan and fry for 1 minute. Put to one side and keep warm.

**4** Add the curry paste to the pan with 75g (3oz) peanuts and fry for 1 minute. Add the noodles and fry for 1 minute. Stir in the coconut milk and toss the noodles over a high heat for 30 seconds.

**5** Put the chicken and spring onions on the coconut noodles. Scatter with the remaining peanuts and serve.

## Cook's Tip

-------------------------------------------------------

**Coconut milk** gives a thick creaminess to stir-fries, soups and curries.

| Serves | EASY | | NUTRITIONAL INFORMATION | |
|---|---|---|---|---|
| **6** | **Preparation Time** 15–20 minutes | **Cooking Time** 15 minutes | **Per Serving** 580 calories, 29g fat (of which 8g saturates), 37g carbohydrate, 3.2g salt | Dairy free |

## Try Something Different

------------------------------------------------

**Replace the chicken** with thinly sliced turkey escalopes. Increase the heat of the dish by frying a chopped chilli with the garlic and ginger.

# Chicken with Vegetables and Noodles

225g (8oz) fine egg noodles

about 2 tbsp vegetable oil

1 skinless chicken breast fillet, cut into very thin strips

2.5cm (1in) piece fresh root ginger, peeled and finely chopped

1 garlic clove, finely chopped

1 red pepper, seeded and thinly sliced

4 spring onions, thinly sliced, plus extra to garnish

2 carrots, thinly sliced

125g (4oz) shiitake or button mushrooms, halved

a handful of bean sprouts (optional)

3 tbsp hoisin sauce

2 tbsp light soy sauce

1 tbsp chilli sauce

sesame seeds to garnish

**1** Bring a large pan of water to the boil and cook the noodles for about 3 minutes or according to the pack instructions. Drain thoroughly and toss with a little of the oil to prevent them sticking together; set aside.

**2** Heat the remaining oil in a wok or large frying pan. Add the chicken, ginger and garlic and cook over a very high heat until the chicken is browned on the outside and cooked right through (about 5 minutes).

**3** Add all the vegetables to the pan and stir-fry over a high heat for about 2 minutes or until they are just cooked, but still crunchy.

**4** Stir in the hoisin sauce, soy sauce and chilli sauce and mix well. Add the noodles, toss well to mix and cook for a couple of minutes until heated through. Serve immediately, sprinkled with shredded spring onion and sesame seeds.

| Serves 2 | EASY | | NUTRITIONAL INFORMATION | |
|---|---|---|---|---|
| | **Preparation Time** 10 minutes | **Cooking Time** About 12 minutes | **Per Serving** 584 calories, 19g fat (of which 3g saturates), 67g carbohydrate, 4.1g salt | Dairy free |

# Thai Chicken and Noodle Soup

1 tbsp olive oil

300g (11oz) boneless, skinless chicken thighs, cubed

3 garlic cloves, crushed

2 medium red chillies, seeded and finely diced (see page 23)

1 litre (1¾ pints) chicken stock

250g (9oz) each green beans, broccoli, sugarsnap peas and courgettes, sliced

50g (2oz) vermicelli or spaghetti, broken into short lengths

**1** Heat the oil in a large pan, add the chicken, garlic and chillies and cook for 5–10 minutes until the chicken is opaque all over.

**2** Add the stock and bring to the boil, then add the vegetables and simmer for 5 minutes or until the chicken is cooked through.

**3** Meanwhile, cook the pasta in a separate pan of lightly salted boiling water for 5–10 minutes until al dente, depending on the type of pasta.

**4** Drain the pasta, add to the broth, and serve immediately.

| A LITTLE EFFORT | | NUTRITIONAL INFORMATION | | Serves |
|---|---|---|---|---|
| **Preparation Time** 30 minutes | **Cooking Time** 15 minutes | **Per Serving** 229 calories, 7g fat (of which 1g saturates), 16g carbohydrate, 1.2g salt | Dairy free | **4** |

3 tbsp dark soy sauce

1 tbsp dry sherry

1 tsp sesame oil

225g (8oz) duck breast fillets, thinly sliced

1 tbsp sugar

2 tsp cornflour

3 tbsp distilled malt vinegar

1 tbsp tomato ketchup

4 tbsp vegetable oil

125g (4oz) aubergine, sliced

1 red onion, sliced

1 garlic clove, sliced

125g (4oz) carrot, sliced lengthways into strips

125g (4oz) sugarsnap peas or mangetouts

1 mango, peeled, stoned and thinly sliced

noodles to serve

# Sweet and Sour Duck

**1** Mix 1 tbsp soy sauce with the sherry and sesame oil. Pour the mixture over the duck, cover and leave to marinate for at least 30 minutes.

**2** Mix together the sugar, cornflour, vinegar, ketchup and remaining 2 tbsp soy sauce. Put to one side.

**3** Heat 2 tbsp vegetable oil in a wok or large non-stick frying pan. Drain the duck from the marinade and reserve the marinade. Fry the duck slices over a high heat for 3–4 minutes until golden and the fat is crisp. Remove from the pan and put to one side.

**4** Add 1 tbsp vegetable oil to the pan and fry the aubergine for about 2 minutes on each side, or until golden. Add the remaining 1 tbsp oil and fry the onion, garlic and carrot for 2–3 minutes, then add the sugarsnap peas or mangetouts and fry for a further 1–2 minutes.

**5** Add the mango to the pan along with the duck, the soy sauce mixture and the reserved marinade. Bring to the boil, stirring gently all the time, and allow to bubble for 2–3 minutes until slightly thickened. Serve immediately, with noodles.

| Serves 4 | EASY | | NUTRITIONAL INFORMATION | |
|---|---|---|---|---|
| | **Preparation Time** 15 minutes, plus marinating | **Cooking Time** About 15 minutes | **Per Serving** 278 calories, 13g fat (of which 2g saturates), 29g carbohydrate, 1.9g salt | Dairy free |

# Turkey and Sesame Stir-fry with Noodles

300g (11oz) turkey breast fillets, cut into thin strips

3 tbsp teriyaki marinade

3 tbsp clear honey

500g (1lb 2oz) medium egg noodles

about 1 tbsp sesame oil, plus extra for the noodles

300g (11oz) ready-prepared mixed stir-fry vegetables, such as carrots, broccoli, red cabbage, mangetouts, bean sprouts and purple spring onions

2 tbsp sesame seeds, lightly toasted in a dry wok or heavy-based pan

**1** Put the turkey strips into a large bowl with the teriyaki marinade and honey, and stir to coat. Cover and put to one side for 5 minutes.

**2** Cook the noodles in boiling water for about 4 minutes or according to the pack instructions. Drain well, then toss in a little oil.

**3** Heat 1 tbsp oil in a wok or large frying pan and add the turkey, reserving the marinade. Stir-fry over a very high heat for 2–3 minutes until cooked through and beginning to brown. Add a drop more oil, if needed, then add the vegetables and reserved marinade. Continue to cook over a high heat, stirring, until the vegetables have started to soften and the sauce is warmed through.

**4** Scatter with the sesame seeds and serve immediately with the noodles.

| EASY | | NUTRITIONAL INFORMATION | | Serves |
|---|---|---|---|---|
| **Preparation Time** 5 minutes, plus marinating | **Cooking Time** 10 minutes | **Per Serving** 672 calories, 18g fat (of which 4g saturates), 97g carbohydrate, 0.7g salt | Dairy free | **4** |

# Chicken Stir-fry with Noodles

2 tbsp vegetable oil

2 garlic cloves, peeled and crushed

4 large skinless, boneless chicken thighs, each sliced into 10 pieces

3 medium carrots, peeled and cut into thin strips

250g pack thick egg noodles

1 bunch spring onions, sliced

200g (7oz) mangetouts, ends trimmed

155g jar sweet chilli and lemongrass sauce

**1** Fill a large pan with water and bring to the boil. Meanwhile, heat the oil in a wok or frying pan, then add the garlic and stir-fry for 1–2 minutes. Add the chicken pieces and stir-fry for 5 minutes, then add the carrot strips and stir-fry for a further 5 minutes.

**2** Put the noodles into the boiling water and cook according to the pack instructions.

**3** Meanwhile, add the spring onions, mangetouts and sauce to the wok and stir-fry for 5 minutes.

**4** Drain the cooked noodles well and add to the wok. Toss everything together and serve.

| EASY | | NUTRITIONAL INFORMATION | | Serves |
|---|---|---|---|---|
| **Preparation Time** 20 minutes | **Cooking Time** 20 minutes | **Per Serving** 355 calories, 10g fat (of which 2g saturates), 29g carbohydrate, 0.5g salt | Dairy free | 4 |

# 4

# Pork

# Ham and Mushroom Pasta

350g (12oz) penne pasta

1 tbsp olive oil

2 shallots, sliced

200g (7oz) small button mushrooms

3 tbsp crème fraîche

125g (4oz) smoked ham, roughly chopped

2 tbsp freshly chopped flat-leafed parsley

salt and ground black pepper

**1** Cook the pasta in a large pan of lightly salted boiling water until al dente.

**2** Meanwhile, heat the oil in a pan. Add the shallots and fry gently for 3 minutes or until starting to soften. Add the mushrooms and fry for 5–6 minutes.

**3** Drain the pasta, put back into the pan and add the shallots and mushrooms. Stir in the crème fraîche, ham and parsley. Toss everything together, season with salt and pepper and heat through to serve.

| Serves | EASY | | NUTRITIONAL INFORMATION |
|---|---|---|---|
| 4 | **Preparation Time** 5 minutes | **Cooking Time** 15 minutes | **Per Serving** 415 calories, 10g fat (of which 4g saturates), 67g carbohydrate, 1g salt |

# Pasta with Leeks, Pancetta and Mushrooms

450g (1lb) dried conchiglie pasta
50g (2oz) butter
125g (4oz) pancetta, diced
2 medium leeks, thickly sliced
225g (8oz) chestnut mushrooms, sliced
1 garlic clove, crushed
150g pack soft cream cheese with herbs
salt and ground black pepper
basil leaves to garnish

**1** Cook the pasta according to the pack instructions until al dente.

**2** Meanwhile, melt the butter in a pan and add the pancetta, leeks, mushrooms and garlic. Cook over a medium heat for 5–10 minutes until the leeks are tender. Reduce the heat, add the cream cheese and season well with salt and pepper.

**3** Drain the pasta, add to the sauce and toss well. Garnish with basil and serve.

| EASY | | NUTRITIONAL INFORMATION | Serves |
|---|---|---|---|
| **Preparation Time** 5 minutes | **Cooking Time** 15–20 minutes | **Per Serving** 765 calories, 39g fat (of which 22g saturates), 86g carbohydrate, 1.5g salt | **4** |

# Spiced Pork with Lemon Pasta

8 thick pork sausages

500g (1lb 2oz) dried pasta shells or other shapes

100ml (3½fl oz) dry white wine

grated zest of 1 lemon

juice of ½ lemon

large pinch of dried chilli flakes

300ml (½ pint) half-fat crème fraîche

2 tbsp freshly chopped flat-leafed parsley

25g (1oz) Parmesan, freshly grated

salt and ground black pepper

**1** Remove the skin from the sausages and pinch the meat into small pieces. Heat a non-stick frying pan over a medium heat. When hot, add the sausagemeat and cook for 5 minutes, stirring occasionally, until cooked through and browned.

**2** Meanwhile, cook the pasta according to the pack instructions until al dente.

**3** Add the wine to the sausagemeat, bring to the boil and let bubble, stirring, for 2–3 minutes until the liquid has reduced right down. Add the lemon zest and juice, chilli flakes and crème fraîche. Season well with salt and pepper. Continue to cook for 3–4 minutes until reduced and thickened slightly.

**4** Drain the pasta and return to the pan. Stir the parsley into the sauce and toss with the pasta. Serve immediately, with Parmesan.

| Serves 6 | EASY | | NUTRITIONAL INFORMATION |
|---|---|---|---|
| | **Preparation Time** 10 minutes | **Cooking Time** 12 minutes | **Per Serving** 733 calories, 44g fat (of which 28g saturates), 71g carbohydrate, 1.8g salt |

# Bacon, Chilli and Herb Pasta

400g (14oz) dried fusilli pasta

150g (5oz) smoked streaky bacon, chopped

50g (2oz) butter

1 tbsp finely chopped fresh parsley or sage

½ red chilli, seeded and finely chopped (see page 23)

salt and ground black pepper

**1** Cook the pasta in a large pan of lightly salted boiling water according to the pack instructions.

**2** Heat a large pan and fry the bacon for 3 minutes.

**3** Add the butter, sage and chilli, and cook for 30 seconds. Season with pepper.

**4** Drain the pasta and tip into a bowl, then stir the sauce into the pasta and serve.

| Serves | EASY | | NUTRITIONAL INFORMATION |
|--------|------|------|------------------------|
| 4 | **Preparation Time** 5 minutes | **Cooking Time** 10 minutes | **Per Serving** 545 calories, 21g fat (of which 10g saturates), 76g carbohydrate, 1.4g salt |

## Cook's Tip

--------------------------------------------------

**To prepare ahead**, complete the recipe to the end of step 2, cool quickly, cover and chill for up to one day.
**To use**, bring back to the boil, stir in the pasta and complete the recipe.

# Spicy Salami and Pasta Supper

1 tbsp olive oil

200g (7oz) salami, sliced

225g (8oz) onion, finely chopped

50g (2oz) celery, finely chopped

2 garlic cloves, crushed

400g can pimientos, drained, rinsed and chopped

400g (14oz) passata or 400g can chopped tomatoes

125g (4oz) sun-dried tomatoes in oil, drained

600ml (1 pint) hot chicken or vegetable stock

300ml (½ pint) red wine

1 tbsp sugar

75g (3oz) pasta shapes

400g can borlotti beans, drained and rinsed

salt and ground black pepper

freshly chopped flat-leafed parsley to garnish

300ml (½ pint) soured cream and 175g (6oz) freshly grated Parmesan, to serve

**1** Heat the oil in a large pan over a medium heat and fry the salami for 5 minutes or until golden and crisp. Drain on kitchen paper.

**2** Fry the onion and celery in the hot oil for 10 minutes or until soft and golden. Add the garlic and fry for 1 minute. Put the salami back in the pan with the pimientos, passata or chopped tomatoes, the sun-dried tomatoes, hot stock, wine and sugar and bring to the boil.

**3** Stir in the pasta, bring back to the boil and cook for about 10 minutes, or according to the pack instructions, until the pasta is almost tender.

**4** Stir in the beans and simmer for 3–4 minutes. Top up with more stock if the pasta is not tender when the liquid has been absorbed. Season with salt and pepper.

**5** Ladle into warmed bowls and serve topped with soured cream and garnished with chopped parsley. Serve the grated Parmesan separately.

| EASY | | NUTRITIONAL INFORMATION | Serves |
|---|---|---|---|
| **Preparation Time** 15 minutes | **Cooking Time** 30 minutes | **Per Serving** 629 calories, 39g fat (of which 18g saturates), 36g carbohydrate, 3.1g salt | **6** |

# Pork and Chilli Noodle Soup

1 tbsp vegetable oil

400g (14oz) pork fillet, cut into thin strips

¼ red chilli, finely chopped (see page 23)

2.5cm (1in) piece fresh root ginger, peeled and cut into slivers

½ tsp smoked paprika

1 red pepper, seeded and thinly sliced

400ml can coconut milk

700ml (1 pint 3½fl oz) hot chicken stock

175g (6oz) medium egg noodles

50g (2oz) spinach

a large handful of fresh coriander, roughly chopped

**1** Heat the oil in a pan and fry the meat in two batches until golden. Add the chilli, ginger, paprika and sliced pepper and cook for a further minute.

**2** Add the coconut milk and hot stock and simmer for 5 minutes. Stir in the noodles and cook for 4 minutes.

**3** Divide among four warmed bowls, scatter the spinach and coriander on top and serve.

| EASY | | NUTRITIONAL INFORMATION | | Serves |
|---|---|---|---|---|
| **Preparation Time** 10 minutes | **Cooking Time** 10 minutes | **Per Serving** 359 calories, 11g fat (of which 3g saturates), 39g carbohydrate, 0.7g salt | Dairy free | **4** |

## Cook's Tip

---

**The smaller the chilli,** the hotter it is.

# Pork Stir-fry with Chilli and Mango

75g (3oz) medium egg noodles

1 tsp groundnut oil

½ red chilli, seeded and finely chopped (see Cook's Tip and page 23)

125g (4oz) pork stir-fry strips

1 head pak choi, roughly chopped

1 tbsp soy sauce

½ ripe mango, peeled, stoned and sliced

**1** Cook the egg noodles in boiling water according to the pack instructions. Drain, then plunge into cold water and put to one side.

**2** Meanwhile, put the oil into a wok or large frying pan and heat until very hot. Add the chilli and pork, and stir-fry for 3–4 minutes. Add the pak choi and soy sauce, and cook for a further 2–3 minutes. Add the mango and toss to combine.

**3** Drain the noodles and add to the pan. Toss well and cook for 1–2 minutes until heated through. Serve immediately.

| Serves | EASY | | NUTRITIONAL INFORMATION | |
|---|---|---|---|---|
| 1 | **Preparation Time** 5 minutes | **Cooking Time** 10 minutes | **Per Serving** 550 calories, 15g fat (of which 4g saturates), 67g carbohydrate, 3.1g salt | Dairy free |

## Try Something Different

----------------------------------------------------

**Instead of fish sauce,** season with a little salt to taste.
**Instead of sugarsnap peas,** use frozen peas.

# Pork and Noodle Stir-fry

1 tbsp sesame oil

5cm (2in) piece fresh root ginger, peeled and grated

2 tbsp soy sauce

1 tbsp fish sauce

½ red chilli, finely chopped (see page 23)

450g (1lb) stir-fry pork strips

2 red peppers, seeded and roughly chopped

250g (9oz) baby sweetcorn, halved lengthways

200g (7oz) sugarsnap peas, halved

300g (11oz) bean sprouts

250g (9oz) rice noodles

**1** Put the sesame oil into a large bowl. Add the ginger, soy sauce, fish sauce, chilli and pork strips. Mix well and leave to marinate for 10 minutes.

**2** Heat a wok or large frying pan until hot. Lift the pork out of the marinade with a slotted spoon and add it to the pan. Stir-fry over a high heat for 5 minutes. Add the peppers, sweetcorn, sugarsnap peas, bean sprouts and remaining marinade and stir-fry for a further 2–3 minutes until the pork is cooked.

**3** Meanwhile, soak the noodles for 4 minutes or according to the pack instructions.

**4** Drain the noodles, add them to the pan and toss well. Serve immediately.

| EASY | | NUTRITIONAL INFORMATION | | Serves |
|---|---|---|---|---|
| **Preparation Time** 15 minutes, plus marinating | **Cooking Time** 7–8 minutes | **Per Serving** 476 calories, 8g fat (of which 2g saturates), 64g carbohydrate, 3.4g salt | Dairy free | **4** |

# Twice-cooked Pork with Black Bean Sauce

700g (1½b) belly pork rashers

2 tbsp vegetable oil

1 garlic clove, crushed

1cm (½in) piece fresh root ginger, peeled and finely chopped

1 onion, quartered lengthways, halved crossways and separated into layers

4 spring onions, cut into 2.5cm (1in) pieces

½ red pepper, seeded and cut into 1cm (½in) squares

½ yellow pepper, seeded and cut into 1cm (½in) squares

½ orange pepper, seeded and cut into 1cm (½in) squares

1 tbsp light soy sauce

1 tbsp dry sherry

150g (5oz) black bean sauce

noodles to serve

**1** Cook the belly pork rashers in boiling water for 30 minutes. Drain well and leave to cool. Remove the rinds and any bones and cut the rashers into 2.5cm (1in) pieces.

**2** Heat the oil in a wok or large frying pan, add the pork and stir-fry for 3–4 minutes until crisp and light golden.

**3** Add the garlic, ginger, onion, spring onions and peppers to the pan and stir-fry for 2 minutes. Add the soy sauce, sherry and black bean sauce and stir-fry for 1–2 minutes until heated through. Serve immediately, with noodles.

| Serves 4 | EASY | | NUTRITIONAL INFORMATION | |
|---|---|---|---|---|
| | **Preparation Time** 12 minutes | **Cooking Time** About 40 minutes | **Per Serving** 548 calories, 39g fat (of which 12g saturates), 13g carbohydrate, 2.7g salt | Dairy free |

## Freezing Tip

**To freeze** Complete the recipe to the end of step 4. Add the pasta and cook for 10 minutes – it will continue to cook right through when you reheat the Bolognese. Cool, put into a freezer-proof container and freeze for up to three months.

**To use** Thaw overnight at a cool room temperature, put into a pan and add 150ml (¼ pint) water. Bring to the boil, then simmer gently for 10 minutes or until the sauce is hot and the pasta is cooked.

3 tbsp olive oil

2 large red onions, finely diced

a few fresh rosemary sprigs

1 large aubergine, finely diced

8 plump coarse sausages

350ml (12fl oz) full-bodied red wine

700g (1½ lb) passata

4 tbsp sun-dried tomato paste

300ml (½ pint) hot vegetable stock

175g (6oz) small pasta, such as orecchiette

salt and ground black pepper

# Chunky One-pot Bolognese

**1** Heat 2 tbsp oil in a large, shallow, non-stick pan. Add the onions and rosemary and cook over a gentle heat for 10 minutes or until soft and golden.

**2** Add the aubergine and remaining oil and cook over a medium heat for 8–10 minutes until soft and golden.

**3** Meanwhile, pull the skin off the sausages and divide each into four rough chunks. Tip the aubergine mixture on to a plate and add the sausage chunks to the hot pan. You won't need any extra oil.

**4** Stir the sausage pieces over a high heat for 6–8 minutes until golden and beginning to turn crisp at the edges. Pour in the wine and let it bubble for 6–8 minutes, until only a little liquid remains. Put the aubergine mixture back into the pan, along with the passata, tomato paste and hot stock.

**5** Stir the pasta into the liquid and cover the pan, then simmer for 20 minutes or until the pasta is cooked. Taste and season with salt and pepper if necessary.

| EASY | | NUTRITIONAL INFORMATION | | Serves |
|---|---|---|---|---|
| **Preparation Time** 15 minutes | **Cooking Time** About 1 hour | **Per Serving** 506 calories, 31g fat (of which 11g saturates), 40g carbohydrate, 1.5g salt | Dairy free | 6 |

# 5

# Beef and Lamb

1 half leg of lamb roasting joint – about 1.1kg (2½lb) total weight

125g (4oz) smoked streaky bacon, chopped

150ml (¼ pint) red wine

400g can chopped tomatoes with chilli, or 400g (14oz) passata

75g (3oz) pasta shapes

12 sunblush tomatoes

150g (5oz) chargrilled artichokes in oil, drained and halved

a handful of basil leaves to garnish

# Lamb and Pasta Pot

**1** Preheat the oven to 200°C (180°C fan oven) mark 6. Put the lamb and bacon into a small, deep roasting tin and fry for 5 minutes or until the lamb is brown all over and the bacon is beginning to crisp.

**2** Remove the lamb and put to one side. Pour the wine into the tin with the bacon – it should bubble immediately. Stir well, scraping the base to loosen any crusty bits, then leave to bubble until half the wine has evaporated. Stir in 300ml (½ pint) water and add the chopped tomatoes or passata, the pasta and sunblush tomatoes.

**3** Put the lamb on a rack over the roasting tin so that the juices drip into the pasta. Cook, uncovered, in the oven for about 35 minutes.

**4** Stir the artichokes into the pasta and put everything back in the oven for 5 minutes, or until the lamb is tender and the pasta cooked. Slice the lamb thickly and serve with the pasta, garnished with the basil.

| Serves 4 | EASY | | NUTRITIONAL INFORMATION | |
|---|---|---|---|---|
| | **Preparation Time** 10 minutes | **Cooking Time** 50 minutes | **Per Serving** 686 calories, 36g fat (of which 16g saturates), 18g carbohydrate, 1.4g salt | Dairy free |

## Cook's Tip

**Look out for** bags of dried porcini pieces in supermarkets. These chopped dried mushrooms are ideal for adding a rich depth of flavour to stews or casseroles.

# Italian Lamb Stew

2 half legs of lamb (knuckle ends)

2 tbsp olive oil

75g (3oz) butter

275g (10oz) onions, finely chopped

175g (6oz) carrots, finely chopped

175g (6oz) celery, finely chopped

2 tbsp dried porcini pieces (see Cook's Tip) or 125g (4oz) brown-cap mushrooms, finely chopped

9 pieces sun-dried tomato, finely chopped

150g (5oz) Italian-style spicy sausage or salami, thickly sliced

600ml (1 pint) red wine

400g (14oz) passata

600ml (1 pint) vegetable stock

125g (4oz) pasta shapes

15g (½oz) freshly grated Parmesan

freshly chopped flat-leafed parsley to garnish

**1** Preheat the oven to 240°C (220°C fan oven) mark 9. Put the lamb in a large roasting tin and drizzle 1 tbsp oil over it. Roast for 35 minutes.

**2** Meanwhile, melt the butter with the remaining oil in a large flameproof casserole. Stir in the onions, carrots and celery and cook, stirring, for 10–15 minutes until soft. Stir in the porcini pieces; cook for 2–3 minutes. Add the sun-dried tomatoes, sausage, wine, passata and stock, bring to the boil, then reduce the heat and simmer for 10 minutes.

**3** Lift the lamb from the tin, add to the casserole and cover with a tight-fitting lid. Reduce the oven temperature to 170°C (150°C fan oven) mark 3; cook for 3 hours or until the lamb is falling off the bone.

**4** Lift the lamb from the casserole and put on a deep, heatproof serving dish. Cover loosely with foil and keep warm in a low oven.

**5** Put the casserole on the hob, add the pasta and bring back to the boil. Reduce the heat and simmer until the pasta is tender. Stir in the Parmesan just before serving. Carve the lamb into large pieces and serve with the pasta sauce, garnished with parsley.

| EASY | | NUTRITIONAL INFORMATION | Serves |
|---|---|---|---|
| **Preparation Time** 35 minutes | **Cooking Time** 3 hours 45 minutes | **Per Serving** 824 calories, 41g fat (of which 12g saturates), 25g carbohydrate, 1.8g salt | **6** |

# Cannelloni with Roasted Garlic

20 garlic cloves, unpeeled

2 tbsp extra virgin olive oil

15g (½oz) dried porcini mushrooms, soaked for 20 minutes in 150ml (¼ pint) boiling water

5 shallots or button onions, finely chopped

700g (1½lb) lean minced meat

175ml (6fl oz) beef or lamb stock

2 tbsp freshly chopped thyme

about 12 lasagne sheets

142ml carton single cream mixed with 2 tbsp sun-dried tomato paste

butter to grease

75g (3oz) Gruyère cheese, finely grated

salt and ground black pepper

**1** Preheat the oven to 180°C (160°C fan oven) mark 4. Put the garlic into a small roasting tin with 1 tbsp oil. Toss to coat the garlic in the oil and cook for 25 minutes or until soft. Leave to cool.

**2** Meanwhile, drain the porcini mushrooms, putting the liquor to one side, then rinse to remove any grit. Chop the mushrooms finely.

**3** Heat the remaining oil in a pan. Add the shallots and cook over a medium heat for 5 minutes or until soft. Increase the heat and stir in the meat. Cook, stirring frequently, until browned. Add the stock, the mushrooms with their liquor, and the thyme. Cook over a medium heat for 15–20 minutes until the liquid has almost evaporated. The mixture should be quite moist. Peel the garlic cloves and mash them to a rough paste with a fork. Stir into the meat mixture, then season with salt and pepper, and set aside.

**4** Cook the lasagne according to the pack instructions until al dente. Drain, rinse with cold water and drain again. Lay each lasagne sheet on a clean teatowel. Spoon the meat mixture along one long edge and roll up to enclose the filling. Cut the tubes in half.

**5** Season the cream and sun-dried tomato paste mixture. Preheat the oven to 200°C (180°C fan oven) mark 6. Grease a shallow baking dish. Arrange a layer of filled tubes in the base of the dish. Spoon half the tomato cream over them and sprinkle with half the cheese. Arrange the remaining tubes on top and cover with the remaining tomato cream and cheese. Cover the dish with foil and cook in the oven for 10 minutes. Uncover and cook for a further 5–10 minutes until lightly browned, then serve.

| Serves | A LITTLE EFFORT | | NUTRITIONAL INFORMATION |
|---|---|---|---|
| 6 | **Preparation Time**<br>40 minutes | **Cooking Time**<br>About 1 hour | **Per Serving**<br>504 calories, 26g fat (of which 11g saturates), 35g carbohydrate, 1.1g salt |

# Beef Chow Mein

2 tsp dark soy sauce

4 tsp dry sherry

1 tsp cornflour

1 tsp sugar

1 tbsp sesame oil

225g (8oz) rump steak, cut into thin strips about 7.5cm (3in) long

175g (6oz) egg noodles

3 tbsp vegetable oil

1 bunch of spring onions, sliced

3 garlic cloves, crushed

1 large green chilli, seeded and sliced (see page 23)

125g (4oz) Chinese leaves, or cabbage, sliced

50g (2oz) bean sprouts

salt and ground black pepper

**1** Put the soy sauce, sherry, cornflour, sugar and 1 tsp sesame oil into a bowl and whisk together. Pour this mixture over the beef, then cover, chill and leave to marinate for at least 1 hour or overnight.

**2** Cook the noodles in boiling water for 4 minutes or according to the pack instructions. Rinse in cold water and drain.

**3** Drain the beef, reserving the marinade. Heat the vegetable oil in a wok or large non-stick frying pan and fry the beef over a high heat until well browned. Remove with a slotted spoon and put to one side.

**4** Add the spring onions, garlic, chilli, Chinese leaves or cabbage and the bean sprouts to the pan and stir-fry for 2–3 minutes. Return the beef to the pan with the noodles and reserved marinade. Bring to the boil, stirring all the time, and bubble for 2–3 minutes. Sprinkle the remaining sesame oil over it, season with salt and pepper and serve immediately.

| EASY | | NUTRITIONAL INFORMATION | | Serves |
|---|---|---|---|---|
| **Preparation Time** 15 minutes, plus marinating | **Cooking Time** 15 minutes | **Per Serving** 408 calories, 20g fat (of which 5g saturates), 38g carbohydrate, 1.2g salt | Dairy free | **4** |

2 rump steaks, about 175g (6oz) each, trimmed

1 tsp vegetable oil

300g pack straight-to-wok noodles

1 red pepper, seeded and thinly sliced

300g (11oz) cabbage, shredded

2 carrots, cut into matchsticks

150g (5oz) shiitake mushrooms, sliced

300g (11oz) bean sprouts

# Marinated Beef and Vegetable Stir-fry

**For the sauce**

1 red chilli, finely chopped (see page 23)

1 garlic clove, finely chopped

2 tbsp soy sauce

2 tbsp sweet chilli sauce

juice of 1 lime

**1** First, make the sauce. Put all the sauce ingredients in a large, shallow bowl and mix well. Add the steaks and turn to coat. Cover and chill in the refrigerator for up to 24 hours, if you like.

**2** Heat the oil in a wok or large frying pan over a high heat. Remove the steaks from the sauce, reserving the sauce, and cook them for 1–2 minutes on each side. Remove from the pan and set aside.

**3** Add the noodles, red pepper, cabbage, carrots and mushrooms to the pan and stir-fry over a high heat for 2–3 minutes. Add the bean sprouts and the reserved sauce and stir-fry for a further 2–3 minutes.

**4** Thinly slice the steak and add it to the pan. Toss everything together and serve immediately.

| Serves | EASY | | NUTRITIONAL INFORMATION | |
|---|---|---|---|---|
| **4** | **Preparation Time** 15 minutes, plus up to 24 hours' chilling | **Cooking Time** About 10 minutes | **Per Serving** 543 calories, 15g fat (of which 4g saturates), 74g carbohydrate, 1.8g salt | Dairy free |

# Szechuan Beef

350g (12oz) beef skirt or rump steak, cut into thin strips

5 tbsp hoisin sauce

4 tbsp dry sherry

2 tbsp vegetable oil

2 red or green chillies, finely chopped (see page 23)

1 large onion, thinly sliced

2 garlic cloves, crushed

2 red peppers, seeded and cut into diamond shapes

2.5cm (1in) piece fresh root ginger, peeled and grated

225g can bamboo shoots, drained and sliced

1 tbsp sesame oil

**1** Put the beef in a bowl, add the hoisin sauce and sherry and stir to coat. Cover and leave to marinate for 30 minutes.

**2** Heat the vegetable oil in a wok or large frying pan until smoking hot. Add the chillies, onion and garlic and stir-fry over a medium heat for 3–4 minutes until softened. Remove with a slotted spoon and set aside. Add the red peppers, increase the heat and stir-fry for a few seconds. Remove and set aside.

**3** Add the steak and marinade to the pan in batches. Stir-fry each batch over a high heat for about 1 minute, removing with a slotted spoon.

**4** Return the vegetables to the pan. Add the ginger and bamboo shoots, then the beef, and stir-fry for a further 1 minute until heated through. Transfer to a warmed serving dish, sprinkle the sesame oil over the top and serve immediately.

| EASY | | NUTRITIONAL INFORMATION | | Serves |
|---|---|---|---|---|
| **Preparation Time** 15 minutes, plus marinating | **Cooking Time** 5–10 minutes | **Per Serving** 298 calories, 14g fat (of which 4g saturates), 15g carbohydrate, 0.6g salt | Dairy free | **4** |

# Sweet Chilli Beef Stir-fry

1 tsp chilli oil

1 tbsp soy sauce

1 tbsp clear honey

1 garlic clove, crushed

1 large red chilli, seeded and chopped (see page 23)

400g (14oz) lean beef, cut into strips

1 tsp sunflower oil

1 broccoli head, shredded

200g (7oz) mangetouts, halved

1 red pepper, seeded and cut into strips

soba noodles or rice to serve

**1** Put the chilli oil, soy sauce, honey, garlic and chilli in a shallow bowl and stir well. Add the strips of beef and toss in the marinade.

**2** Heat the oil in a wok or large frying pan over a high heat until it is very hot. Fry the strips of beef in two batches, cooking each batch for 2–3 minutes until tender. Remove the beef from the pan and set aside. Wipe the pan with kitchen paper to remove any residue.

**3** Add the broccoli, mangetouts, red pepper and 2 tbsp water to the pan. Stir-fry for 5–6 minutes until the vegetables start to soften. Return the beef to the pan and cook until heated through. Serve immediately, with noodles or rice.

| Serves | EASY | | NUTRITIONAL INFORMATION | |
|---|---|---|---|---|
| **4** | **Preparation Time** 10 minutes | **Cooking Time** 10–11 minutes | **Per Serving** 271 calories, 12g fat (of which 4g saturates), 10g carbohydrate, 0.9g salt | Dairy free |

## Try Something Different

--------------------------------------------------

**Use 400g (14oz) pork** escalope cut into strips instead of beef. Cook for 5 minutes; remove from the pan at step 2. **Instead of pak choi**, use Chinese leaves or shredded spring greens or cabbage.

2 tbsp soy sauce

2 tbsp Worcestershire sauce

2 tsp tomato purée

juice of ½ lemon

1 tbsp sesame seeds

1 garlic clove, crushed

400g (14oz) rump steak, sliced

1 tbsp vegetable oil

3 small pak choi, chopped

1 bunch of spring onions, sliced

freshly cooked egg noodles or tagliatelle to serve

# Sesame Beef

**1** Put the soy sauce and Worcestershire sauce, tomato purée, lemon juice, sesame seeds and garlic into a bowl. Add the steak and toss to coat.

**2** Heat the oil in a large wok or non-stick frying pan until hot. Add the steak and sear well. Remove from the wok and set aside.

**3** Add any sauce from the bowl to the wok and heat for 1 minute. Add the pak choi, spring onions and steak and stir-fry for 5 minutes. Add freshly cooked and drained noodles, toss and serve immediately.

| EASY | | NUTRITIONAL INFORMATION | | Serves |
|---|---|---|---|---|
| **Preparation Time** 10 minutes | **Cooking Time** 10 minutes | **Per Serving** 207 calories, 10g fat (of which 3g saturates), 4g carbohydrate, 2g salt | Dairy free | **4** |

# 6

# Vegetarian Dishes

# Pappardelle with Spinach

350g (12oz) pappardelle pasta

350g (12oz) baby leaf spinach, roughly chopped

2 tbsp olive oil

75g (3oz) ricotta cheese

freshly grated nutmeg

salt and ground black pepper

**1** Cook the pappardelle in a large pan of lightly salted boiling water, according to the pack instructions, until al dente.

**2** Drain the pasta well, return to the pan and add the spinach, oil and ricotta, tossing for 10–15 seconds until the spinach has wilted. Season with a little nutmeg, salt and pepper and serve immediately.

| Serves 4 | EASY | | NUTRITIONAL INFORMATION | |
|---|---|---|---|---|
| | **Preparation Time** 5 minutes | **Cooking Time** 12 minutes | **Per Serving** 404 calories, 11g fat (of which 3g saturates), 67g carbohydrate, 0.3g salt | Vegetarian |

# Fusilli with Chilli and Tomatoes

350g (12oz) fusilli or other short dried pasta

4 tbsp olive oil

1 large red chilli, seeded and finely chopped (see page 23)

1 garlic clove, peeled and crushed

500g (1lb 2oz) cherry tomatoes

2 tbsp freshly chopped basil

50g (2oz) Parmesan, shaved (see Cook's Tips)

salt and ground black pepper

**1** Cook the pasta in a large pan of lightly salted boiling water according to the pack instructions. Drain.

**2** Meanwhile, heat the oil in a large frying pan over a high heat. Add the chilli and garlic and cook for 30 seconds. Add the tomatoes, season with salt and pepper, and cook over a high heat for 3 minutes or until the skins begin to split.

**3** Add the basil and drained pasta and toss together. Transfer to a dish, sprinkle the Parmesan shavings over the top and serve immediately.

## Cook's Tips

**Make Parmesan shavings** with a vegetable peeler. Hold the piece of cheese in one hand and pare off wafer-thin strips of cheese using the peeler.

**Genuine Parmesan cheese** is not vegetarian, as it is made with animal rennet. If preparing this dish for strict vegetarians, there are substitutes available.

| EASY | | NUTRITIONAL INFORMATION | | Serves |
|---|---|---|---|---|
| **Preparation Time** 10 minutes | **Cooking Time** 10–15 minutes | **Per Serving** 479 calories, 17g fat (of which 4g saturates), 69g carbohydrate, 0.4g salt | Vegetarian | **4** |

# Ribbon Pasta with Courgettes

450g (1lb) pappardelle pasta

2 large courgettes, coarsely grated

1 red chilli, seeded and finely chopped (see page 23)

2 tbsp salted capers, rinsed

1 garlic clove, crushed

4 tbsp pitted black Kalamata olives, roughly chopped

4 tbsp extra virgin olive oil

2 tbsp freshly chopped flat-leafed parsley

salt and ground black pepper

freshly grated Parmesan to serve (see Cook's Tips, page 107)

**1** Cook the pappardelle in a large pan of boiling water until al dente. About 1 minute before the end of the cooking time, add the courgettes, then simmer until the pasta is just cooked.

**2** Meanwhile, put the chilli, capers, garlic, olives and oil in a small pan. Stir over a low heat for 2–3 minutes.

**3** Drain the pasta and put back in the pan. Pour the hot caper mixture on top, mix well and toss with the parsley. Season with salt and pepper and serve immediately with the Parmesan.

## Try Something Different

**If cooking for non-vegetarians**, try this variation. Omit the Parmesan cheese and in step 2, add a 50g can of anchovies, drained and roughly chopped.

| Serves 4 | EASY | | NUTRITIONAL INFORMATION | |
|---|---|---|---|---|
| | **Preparation Time** About 5 minutes | **Cooking Time** 8–10 minutes | **Per Serving** 518 calories, 15g fat (of which 2g saturates), 86g carbohydrate, 1.7g salt | Vegetarian Dairy free |

# Pea, Mint and Ricotta Pasta

300g (11oz) farfalle pasta
200g (7oz) frozen peas
175g (6oz) ricotta cheese
3 tbsp freshly chopped mint
2 tbsp extra virgin olive oil
salt and ground black pepper

**1** Cook the pasta in a large pan of lightly salted boiling water according to the pack instructions. Add the frozen peas for the last 4 minutes of cooking.

**2** Drain the pasta and peas, reserving the water, then return to the pan. Stir in the ricotta and mint with a ladleful of pasta cooking water. Season well, drizzle with the oil and serve at once.

| Serves | EASY | | NUTRITIONAL INFORMATION | |
|---|---|---|---|---|
| 4 | **Preparation Time**<br>5 minutes | **Cooking Time**<br>10 minutes | **Per Serving**<br>431 calories, 14g fat (of which 5g saturates),<br>63g carbohydrate, 0.2g salt | Vegetarian |

## Cook's Tip

**Use leftover cooked pasta,** beans or potatoes: tip the pasta into a pan of boiling water and bring back to the boil for 30 seconds. Bring the beans or potatoes to room temperature, but there's no need to re-boil them.

# Pasta with Pesto and Beans

350g (12oz) dried pasta shapes

175g (6oz) fine green beans, roughly chopped

175g (6oz) small salad potatoes, thickly sliced

250g (9oz) pesto

Parmesan shavings to serve (see Cook's Tips, page 107)

**1** Bring a large pan of lightly salted water to the boil. Add the pasta, bring back to the boil and cook for 5 minutes.

**2** Add the beans and potatoes to the pan and boil for a further 7–8 minutes until the potatoes are just tender.

**3** Drain the pasta, beans and potatoes in a colander, then tip everything back into the pan and stir in the pesto. Serve scattered with Parmesan shavings.

| EASY | | NUTRITIONAL INFORMATION | | Serves |
|---|---|---|---|---|
| **Preparation Time** 5 minutes | **Cooking Time** 15 minutes | **Per Serving** 738 calories, 38g fat (of which 10g saturates), 74g carbohydrate, 1g salt | Vegetarian | **4** |

# Pasta with Pinenuts and Pesto

300g (11oz) penne pasta

50g (2oz) pinenuts

1 tbsp olive oil

1 garlic clove, crushed

250g (9oz) closed cup mushrooms, sliced

2 courgettes, sliced

250g (9oz) cherry tomatoes

6 tbsp fresh pesto

25g (1oz) Parmesan, shaved (see Cook's Tips, page 107)

salt

**1** Cook the pasta according to the pack instructions until al dente.

**2** Meanwhile, gently toast the pinenuts in a frying pan, tossing them around until golden, then remove from the pan and set aside. Add the oil to the pan with the garlic, mushrooms and courgettes. Add a splash of water, then cover and cook for 4–5 minutes.

**3** Uncover and add the tomatoes, then cook for a further 1–2 minutes. Drain the pasta and return to its pan. Add the vegetables, pinenuts and pesto to the drained pasta. Toss well to combine and serve immediately, with shavings of Parmesan.

| Serves | EASY | | NUTRITIONAL INFORMATION | |
|---|---|---|---|---|
| 4 | **Preparation Time** 5 minutes | **Cooking Time** 10 minutes | **Per Serving** 567 calories, 29g fat (of which 5g saturates), 60g carbohydrate, 0.4g salt | Vegetarian |

# Pasta with Goat's Cheese and Tomatoes

300g (11oz) conchiglie pasta
2 tbsp olive oil
1 red pepper, seeded and chopped
1 yellow pepper, seeded and chopped
½ tbsp sun-dried tomato paste
75g (3oz) sunblush tomatoes
75g (3oz) soft goat's cheese
2 tbsp freshly chopped parsley
salt and ground black pepper

**1** Cook the pasta in a large pan of lightly salted boiling water, according to the pack instructions, until al dente.

**2** Meanwhile, heat the oil in a pan and fry the red and yellow peppers for 5–7 minutes until softened and just beginning to brown. Add the tomato paste and cook for a further minute. Add a ladleful of pasta cooking water to the pan and simmer for 1–2 minutes to make a sauce.

**3** Drain the pasta and return to the pan. Pour the sauce on top, then add the tomatoes, goat's cheese and parsley. Toss together until the cheese begins to melt, then season with pepper and serve.

| EASY | | NUTRITIONAL INFORMATION | | Serves |
|---|---|---|---|---|
| **Preparation Time** 5 minutes | **Cooking Time** 10 minutes | **Per Serving** 409 calories, 12g fat (of which 4g saturates), 64g carbohydrate, 0.4g salt | Vegetarian | **4** |

# Pasta Shells with Spinach and Ricotta

450g (1lb) fresh spinach, washed
125g (4oz) ricotta cheese
1 medium egg
a pinch of freshly grated nutmeg
grated zest of ½ lemon
50g (2oz) freshly grated Parmesan (see Cook's Tips, page 107)
225g (8oz) conchiglione pasta shells
½ quantity of Classic Tomato Sauce (see Cook's Tip)
25g (1oz) pinenuts
salt and ground black pepper

1 Put the spinach into a large pan. Cover and cook over a low to medium heat for 2–3 minutes until wilted. Drain, squeeze out the excess liquid and chop finely.

2 Put the spinach into a large bowl with the ricotta and beat in the egg. Stir in the grated nutmeg, lemon zest and 25g (1oz) grated Parmesan and season.

3 Preheat the oven to 200°C (180°C fan oven) mark 6. Meanwhile, cook the pasta according to the pack instructions for oven-baked dishes. Drain well.

4 Spread the Classic Tomato Sauce in the bottom of an 18 × 23cm (7 × 9in) ovenproof dish. Fill the shells with spinach mixture and arrange on top of the sauce. Sprinkle with 25g (1oz) grated Parmesan and the pinenuts. Cook in the oven for 20–25 minutes until golden.

## Cook's Tip

**Classic Tomato Sauce**
Heat 1 tbsp olive oil in a pan. Add 1 small chopped onion, 1 grated carrot and 1 chopped celery stick, then fry gently for 20 minutes until softened. Add 1 crushed garlic clove and ½ tbsp tomato purée and fry for 1 minute. Stir in 2 × 400g cans plum tomatoes, add 1 bay leaf, ½ tsp oregano and 2 tsp caster sugar and simmer for 30 minutes until thickened. Serves 4.

| EASY | | NUTRITIONAL INFORMATION | | Serves |
|---|---|---|---|---|
| **Preparation Time** 10 minutes | **Cooking Time** About 45 minutes | **Per Serving** 430 calories, 17g fat (of which 7g saturates), 50g carbohydrate, 1.6g salt | Vegetarian | 4 |

# Very Easy Four-cheese Gnocchi

350g pack fresh gnocchi

300g tub fresh four-cheese sauce

240g pack sunblush tomatoes

2 tbsp freshly torn basil leaves,
plus basil sprigs to garnish

1 tbsp freshly grated Parmesan (see Cook's Tips,
page 107)

15g (½oz) butter, chopped

salt and ground black pepper

salad to serve

**1** Cook the gnocchi in a large pan of lightly salted boiling water according to the pack instructions, or until all the gnocchi have floated to the surface. Drain well and put the gnocchi back into the pan.

**2** Preheat the grill. Add the four-cheese sauce and tomatoes to the gnocchi and heat gently, stirring, for 2 minutes.

**3** Season with salt and pepper, then add the basil and stir again. Spoon into individual heatproof bowls, sprinkle a little Parmesan over each one and dot with butter.

**4** Cook under the grill for 3–5 minutes until golden and bubbling. Garnish with basil sprigs and serve with salad.

| Serves | EASY | | NUTRITIONAL INFORMATION | |
|---|---|---|---|---|
| 2 | **Preparation Time**<br>3 minutes | **Cooking Time**<br>10 minutes | **Per Serving**<br>630 calories, 28g fat (of which 15g saturates),<br>77g carbohydrate, 5.7g salt | Vegetarian<br>Gluten Free |

# Butternut Squash and Spinach Lasagne

1 butternut squash, peeled, halved, seeded and cut into 3cm (1¼in) cubes

2 tbsp olive oil

1 onion, sliced

25g (1oz) butter

25g (1oz) plain flour

600ml (1 pint) milk

250g (9oz) ricotta cheese

1 tsp freshly grated nutmeg

225g bag baby leaf spinach

6 'no need to pre-cook' lasagne sheets

50g (2oz) pecorino cheese or Parmesan, freshly grated (see Cook's Tips, page 107)

salt and ground black pepper

**1** Preheat the oven to 200°C (180°C fan oven) mark 6. Put the squash into a roasting tin with the oil, onion and 1 tbsp water. Mix well and season with salt and pepper. Roast for 25 minutes, tossing halfway through.

**2** To make the sauce, melt the butter in a pan, then stir in the flour and cook over a medium heat for 1–2 minutes. Gradually add the milk, stirring constantly. Reduce the heat to a simmer and cook, stirring, for 5 minutes or until the sauce has thickened. Crumble the ricotta into the sauce and add the nutmeg. Mix together thoroughly and season with salt and pepper.

**3** Heat 1 tbsp water in a pan. Add the spinach, cover and cook until just wilted. Season generously.

**4** Spoon the squash mixture into a 1.7 litre (3 pint) ovenproof dish. Arrange the spinach on top and cover with a third of the sauce, then the lasagne. Spoon the remaining sauce on top, season and sprinkle with the grated cheese. Cook for 30–35 minutes until the cheese topping is golden and the pasta is cooked.

| Serves 6 | EASY | | NUTRITIONAL INFORMATION | |
|---|---|---|---|---|
| | **Preparation Time** 30 minutes | **Cooking Time** About 1 hour | **Per Serving** 273 calories, 17g fat (of which 7g saturates), 18g carbohydrate, 0.6g salt | Vegetarian |

## Cook's Tip

**Fresh lasagne sheets** wrapped around a filling are used here to make the cannelloni, but you can also buy cannelloni tubes, which can easily be filled using a teaspoon.

# Mixed Mushroom Cannelloni

6 sheets fresh lasagne

3 tbsp olive oil

1 small onion, finely sliced

3 garlic cloves, sliced

20g pack fresh thyme, finely chopped

225g (8oz) chestnut or brown-cap mushrooms, roughly chopped

125g (4oz) flat-cap mushrooms, roughly chopped

2 × 125g goat's cheese logs, with rind

350g carton cheese sauce

salt and ground black pepper

green salad to serve

**1** Preheat the oven to 180°C (160°C fan oven) mark 4. Cook the lasagne in boiling water until just tender. Drain well and run it under cold water to cool. Keep covered with cold water until ready to use.

**2** Heat the oil in a large pan and add the onion. Cook over a medium heat for 7–10 minutes until soft. Add the garlic and fry for 1–2 minutes; put a few slices to one side. Keeping a little thyme for sprinkling, add the rest to the pan with the mushrooms. Cook for 5 minutes, until the mushrooms are golden and there is no liquid in the pan. Season and put to one side.

**3** Crumble one goat's cheese into the cooled mushroom mixture and stir. Drain the lasagne and pat dry with kitchen paper. Spoon 2–3 tbsp of the mushroom mixture along the long edge of each lasagne sheet, leaving a 1cm (½in) border. Roll up the sheets; cut each roll in half. Put in a shallow ovenproof dish and cover with cheese sauce. Slice the remaining goat's cheese into thick rounds and arrange across the pasta rolls. Sprinkle with the reserved garlic and thyme. Cook in the oven for 30–35 minutes until golden and bubbling. Serve with a green salad.

| A LITTLE EFFORT | | NUTRITIONAL INFORMATION | | Serves |
|---|---|---|---|---|
| **Preparation Time** 15 minutes | **Cooking Time** 50–55 minutes | **Per Serving** 631 calories, 37g fat (of which 18g saturates), 50g carbohydrate, 1.9g salt | Vegetarian | **4** |

# Thai Noodles with Tofu

125g (4oz) firm tofu, drained and cut into
2.5cm (1in) cubes

8 shallots, peeled and halved

1 garlic clove, peeled and crushed

2.5cm (1in) piece fresh root ginger, peeled and grated

2 tbsp soy sauce

1 tsp white wine vinegar or rice vinegar

225g (8oz) rice noodles

25g (1oz) unsalted peanuts

2 tbsp sunflower oil

15g (½oz) dried shrimp (if you like)

1 medium egg, beaten

25g (1oz) bean sprouts

fresh basil leaves to garnish (if you like)

### For the sauce

1 dried red chilli, seeded and finely chopped (see
page 23)

2 tbsp lemon juice

1 tbsp Thai fish sauce

1 tbsp caster sugar

2 tbsp smooth peanut butter

**1** Preheat the oven to 200°C (180°C fan oven) mark 6. Put the tofu and shallots into a small roasting pan. Put the garlic, ginger, soy sauce, vinegar and 2 tbsp water into a bowl and stir well. Pour the mixture over the tofu and shallots, and toss well to coat. Roast near the top of the oven for 30 minutes, until the tofu and shallots are golden.

**2** Meanwhile, soak the noodles according to the pack instructions. Drain, refresh under cold running water and set aside. Toast and chop the peanuts.

**3** To make the sauce, put all the ingredients into a small pan and stir over a gentle heat until the sugar dissolves. Keep the sauce warm.

**4** Heat the oil in a wok or large frying pan and stir-fry the dried shrimp, if using, for 1 minute. Add the drained noodles and beaten egg to the pan and stir over a medium heat for 3 minutes. Add the tofu and shallots, together with any pan juices. Stir well, then remove from the heat.

**5** Stir in the bean sprouts and the sauce, then divide among four warmed serving plates. Sprinkle with the toasted peanuts and serve immediately, garnished with basil leaves.

| EASY | | NUTRITIONAL INFORMATION | | Serves |
|---|---|---|---|---|
| **Preparation Time** 25 minutes | **Cooking Time** 35 minutes | **Per Serving** 431 calories, 15g fat (of which 3g saturates), 61g carbohydrate, 2.1g salt | Vegetarian Dairy free | **4** |

vegetable oil for deep-frying

125g (4oz) rice or egg noodles

frisée leaves to serve

**For the sauce**

2 tbsp vegetable oil

1 garlic clove, crushed

1cm (½ in) piece fresh root ginger, peeled and grated

6 spring onions, sliced

½ red pepper, seeded and finely chopped

2 tbsp sugar

2 tbsp malt vinegar

2 tbsp tomato ketchup

2 tbsp dark soy sauce

2 tbsp dry sherry

1 tbsp cornflour

1 tbsp sliced green chillies (see page 23)

# Crispy Noodles with Hot Sweet and Sour Sauce

**1** First, make the sauce. Heat the oil in a wok or large frying pan and stir-fry the garlic, ginger, spring onions and red pepper for 1 minute. Stir in the sugar, vinegar, ketchup, soy sauce and sherry. Blend the cornflour with 8 tbsp water and stir it into the sauce. Cook for 2 minutes, stirring. Add the chillies, cover and keep the sauce warm.

**2** Heat the vegetable oil in a deep-fryer to 190°C (test by frying a small cube of bread; it should brown in 20 seconds). Cut the noodles into six portions and fry, a batch at a time, very briefly until lightly golden (take care as the hot oil rises up quickly).

**3** Drain the noodles on kitchen paper and keep them warm while you cook the remainder.

**4** Arrange the noodles on a bed of frisée leaves and serve immediately, with the sauce served separately.

| Serves 4 | A LITTLE EFFORT | | NUTRITIONAL INFORMATION | |
|---|---|---|---|---|
| | **Preparation Time** 10 minutes | **Cooking Time** About 15 minutes | **Per Serving** 317 calories, 14g fat (of which 2g saturates), 43g carbohydrate, 1.7g salt | Vegetarian Dairy free |

# Sweet Chilli Tofu Stir-fry

200g (7oz) firm tofu

4 tbsp sweet chilli sauce

2 tbsp light soy sauce

1 tbsp sesame seeds

2 tbsp toasted sesame oil

600g (1lb 5oz) ready-prepared mixed stir-fry vegetables, such as carrots, broccoli, mangetouts and bean sprouts

a handful of pea shoots or young salad leaves to garnish

rice to serve

**1** Drain the tofu, pat it dry and cut it into large cubes. Put the tofu into a shallow container and pour 1 tbsp sweet chilli sauce and 1 tbsp light soy sauce over it. Cover and marinate for 10 minutes.

**2** Meanwhile, toast the sesame seeds in a hot wok or large frying pan until golden. Tip on to a plate.

**3** Return the wok or frying pan to the heat and add 1 tbsp sesame oil. Add the marinated tofu and stir-fry for 5 minutes until golden. Remove and set aside.

**4** Heat the remaining 1 tbsp oil in the pan, add the vegetables and stir-fry for 3–4 minutes until just tender. Stir in the cooked tofu.

**5** Pour the remaining sweet chilli sauce and soy sauce into the pan, toss well and cook for a further minute until heated through. Sprinkle with the toasted sesame seeds and pea shoots or salad leaves and serve immediately, with rice.

| EASY | | NUTRITIONAL INFORMATION | | Serves |
|---|---|---|---|---|
| **Preparation Time** 5 minutes, plus marinating | **Cooking Time** 12 minutes | **Per Serving** 167 calories, 11g fat (of which 2g saturates), 5g carbohydrate, 1.6g salt | Vegetarian Dairy free | **4** |

# Tofu Noodle Curry

250g (9oz) fresh tofu

2 tbsp light soy sauce

½ red chilli, chopped (see page 23)

5cm (2in) piece fresh root ginger, peeled and grated

1 tbsp olive oil

1 onion, finely sliced

2 tbsp Thai red curry paste (see Cook's Tip)

200ml (7fl oz) coconut milk

900ml (1½ pints) hot vegetable stock

200g (7oz) baby sweetcorn, halved lengthways

200g (7oz) fine green beans

250g (9oz) medium rice noodles

salt and ground black pepper

2 spring onions, sliced diagonally, and 2 tbsp fresh coriander leaves to garnish

1 lime, cut into wedges, to serve

**1** Drain the tofu, pat it dry and cut it into large cubes. Put the tofu into a shallow dish with the soy sauce, chilli and ginger. Toss to coat, then leave to marinate for 30 minutes.

**2** Heat the oil in a large pan over a medium heat, then add the onion and fry for 10 minutes, stirring, until golden. Add the curry paste and cook for 2 minutes.

**3** Add the tofu and marinade, coconut milk, hot stock and sweetcorn, and season with salt and pepper. Bring to the boil, add the green beans, then reduce the heat and simmer for 8–10 minutes.

**4** Meanwhile, put the noodles into a large bowl, pour boiling water over them and soak for 30 seconds. Drain the noodles, then stir into the curry. Pour into bowls and garnish with the spring onions and coriander. Serve immediately, with lime wedges.

## Cook's Tip

------------------------------------------------------------

**Check the ingredients** in the Thai curry paste: some contain shrimp and are therefore not suitable for vegetarians.

| Serves | EASY | | NUTRITIONAL INFORMATION | |
|---|---|---|---|---|
| 4 | **Preparation Time** 15 minutes, plus marinating | **Cooking Time** About 25 minutes | **Per Serving** 367 calories, 7g fat (of which 1g saturates), 60g carbohydrate, 2g salt | Vegetarian Dairy free |

## Cook's Tip

**Red bird's-eye chillies** are always very hot. The smaller they are, the hotter they are.

# Thai Noodle Salad

200g (7oz) sugarsnap peas, trimmed

250g pack Thai stir-fry rice noodles

100g (3½oz) cashew nuts

300g (11oz) carrots, peeled and cut into batons

10 spring onions, sliced diagonally

300g (11oz) bean sprouts

20g (¾oz) fresh coriander, roughly chopped, plus coriander sprigs to garnish

1 red bird's-eye chilli, seeded and finely chopped (see Cook's Tip and page 23)

2 tsp sweet chilli sauce

4 tbsp sesame oil

6 tbsp soy sauce

juice of 2 limes

salt and ground black pepper

1 Bring a pan of lightly salted water to the boil and blanch the sugarsnap peas for 2–3 minutes until just tender to the bite. Drain and refresh under cold water.

2 Put the noodles into a bowl, cover with boiling water and leave to soak for 4 minutes. Rinse under cold water and drain very well.

3 Toast the cashews in a dry frying pan until golden – about 5 minutes.

4 Put the sugarsnaps in a large glass serving bowl. Add the carrots, spring onions, bean sprouts, chopped coriander, chopped chilli, cashews and noodles. Mix together the chilli sauce, sesame oil, soy sauce and lime juice and season well with salt and pepper. Pour over the salad and toss together, then garnish with coriander sprigs and serve.

| Serves 4 | EASY | | NUTRITIONAL INFORMATION | |
|---|---|---|---|---|
| | **Preparation Time** 20 minutes, plus soaking | **Cooking Time** 7–8 minutes | **Per Serving** 568 calories, 29g fat (of which 4g saturates), 65g carbohydrate, 2.9g salt | Vegetarian Dairy free |

# Index

# Collect the Easy To Makes!...

Good Housekeeping
Slow Cook
easy to make!

Good Housekeeping
Speedy Meals
easy to make!

Good Housekeeping
Chocolate
easy to make!

Good Housekeeping
Chicken
easy to make!

Good Housekeeping
Low GI
easy to make!

Good Housekeeping
Healthy Meals in Minutes
easy to make!

Good Housekeeping
Pies, Pies, Pies
easy to make!

Good Housekeeping
Cakes & Bakes
easy to make!

Good Housekeeping
Soups
easy to make!

Good Housekeeping
Family Meals in Minutes
easy to make!

Good Housekeeping
Wok & Stir-fry
easy to make!

Good Housekeeping
One Pot
easy to make!

Good Housekeeping
Puddings & Desserts
easy to make!

Good Housekeeping
Roasts
easy to make!

Good Housekeeping
Salads & Dressings
easy to make!

Good Housekeeping
Everyday Family Meals
easy to make!

Good Housekeeping
Meat Free
easy to make!

Good Housekeeping
Cupcakes, Muffins and Brownies
easy to make!

Good Housekeeping
BBQ & Grills
easy to make!

Good Housekeeping
Christmas
easy to make!

Good Housekeeping
Pasta & Noodles
easy to make!

Good Housekeeping
Curries & Spicy Meals
easy to make!

Good Housekeeping
Everyday Vegetarian
easy to make!

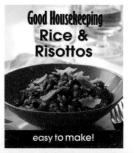
Good Housekeeping
Rice & Risottos
easy to make!

Good Housekeeping Institute
TRIED ★ TESTED ★ TRUSTED